Muslim Women Online

While issues surrounding Muslim women are common in the international media, the voices of Muslim women themselves are largely absent from media coverage and despite the rapidly increasing presence of Muslim women in online groups and discussions, it is still a relatively unexplored topic. This book examines Muslim women in transnational online groups, and their views on education, culture, marriage, sexuality, work, dress-code, race, class and sisterhood.

Looking at both egalitarian and traditionalist Muslim women's views, the author considers their interpretations of Islam and identifies a new category of holists who focus on developing the Islamic sisterhood. Drawing on detailed analysis of online transcripts, she highlights women's rhetorical techniques and the thorough knowledge of Islamic sources which they use to justify their points in online discussions. She details how in the online context, as opposed to offline interactions, Muslim women are much more willing to cross boundaries between traditionalist and egalitarian interpretations of Islam and women's Islamic rights and responsibilities and to develop collaborative interpretations with supporters of different views.

Shedding light on a candid and forthright global community, this book is an important contribution to the debate on women in Islam, and as such will be of interest to scholars and students of Islamic studies, gender studies, media studies and the Middle East.

Anna Piela has a PhD in Women's Studies from the University of York. Her research focuses on interpretations of Islamic texts produced by Muslim women in online spaces, and she has published articles in the *Journal of Muslim Minority Affairs, Contemporary Islam* and *CyberOrient*.

Routledge Islamic Studies Series

This broad ranging series includes books on Islamic issues from all parts of the globe and is not simply confined to the Middle East.

Historians, State and Politics in Twentieth Century Egypt
Contesting the nation
Anthony Gorman

The New Politics of Islam
Pan-Islamic foreign policy in a world of states
Naveed Shahzad Sheikh

The Alevis in Turkey
The emergence of a secular Islamic tradition
David Shankland

Medieval Islamic Economic Thought
Filling the great gap in European economics
S.M. Ghazanfar

The West and Islam
Western liberal democracy versus the system of Shura
Mishal Fahm al-Sulami

The Regency of Tunis and the Ottoman Porte, 1777–1814
Army and government of a North-African Eyâlet at the end of the eighteenth century
Asma Moalla

Islamic Insurance
A modern approach to Islamic banking
Aly Khorshid

The Small Players of the Great Game
The settlement of Iran's eastern borderlands and the creation Afghanistan
Pirouz Mojtahed-Zadeh

Interest in Islamic Economics
Understanding Riba
Abdulkader Thomas

Muslim Diaspora
Gender, culture and identity
Edited by Haideh Moghissi

Human Conscience and Muslim-Christian Relations
Modern Egyptian thinkers on al-ḍamīr
Oddbjørn Leirvik

Islam in Nordic and Baltic Countries
Göran Larsson

Islam and Disability
Perspectives in theology and jurisprudence
Mohammed Ghaly

Producing Islamic Knowledge
Transmission and dissemination in Western Europe
Edited by Martin van Bruinessen and Stefano Allievi

Political Liberalism in Muslim Societies
Fevzi Bilgin

Shari'a Compliant Microfinance
S. Nazim Ali

Muslim Women Online
Faith and identity in virtual space
Anna Piela

Muslim Women Online
Faith and identity in virtual space

Anna Piela

Routledge
Taylor & Francis Group

LONDON AND NEW YORK

First published 2012
by Routledge
2 Park Square, Milton Park, Abingdon, Oxon, OX14 4RN

Simultaneously published in the USA and Canada
by Routledge
711 Third Avenue, New York, NY 10017

Routledge is an imprint of the Taylor & Francis Group, an informa business

© 2012 Anna Piela

British Library Cataloguing in Publication Data
A catalogue record for this book is available from the British Library

Library of Congress Cataloging in Publication Data
Piela, Anna.
Muslim women online: faith and identity in virtual space / Anna Piela.
p. cm. – (Routledge Islamic Studies series)
Includes bibliographical references and index.
1. Feminism–Islamic countries. 2. Muslim women–Islamic countries–Social
conditions. 3. Social networks–Islamic countries. I. Title.
HQ1785.P54 2011
302.23′1088297082–dc22
2011015282

ISBN 978-0-415-59697-8 (hbk)
ISBN 978-0-203-80197-0 (ebk)

Typeset in Times New Roman by GCS, Leighton Buzzard, Bedfordshire

Printed and bound in Great Britain by the MPG Books Group

Contents

Acknowledgements

Doing a PhD is a long and complex process that is never achieved on one's own. This book would never have come into being but for the support of many people whom I would like to thank. First and foremost, I am deeply indebted to both my supervisors, Ann Kaloski-Naylor and Haleh Afshar, for their patient mentoring and support, constructive feedback and friendship during the entire writing process. They have taught me the meaning of academic standards and rigour; by putting their faith in me, they have made this book possible. I am also grateful to Roger Burrows on my Book Advisory Panel as well as to Gabriele Griffin at the Centre for Women's Studies for insightful comments on my work. I also want to specially thank the CWS administrator, Harriet Badger, for four years of assistance and warm support. My heartfelt gratitude goes to my late MA project supervisor, Andrzej Kapiszewski of the Jagiellonian University, whose extensive knowledge, pedagogic talent, and personal integrity contributed to the development of my interest in the study of Islam. I will always remember him as an academic role model whose example also encouraged me to pursue a career in research. I thank Tariq Ramadan and Stevi Jackson for examining my thesis and their subsequent invaluable advice.

This project would not have happened without the input of online group moderators and my research participants, whose online conversations have enlightened me and provided a new perspective, not only on Islamic expressions, but on my own life as well.

I am fortunate to be friends with Jyothsna Beliappa, Julia Carter, Lizzie Guinness, Rosey Hill, Maria Karepova, Kate MacLean, Laura Zahra MacDonald, and Petra Nordqvist. I appreciate their collective encouragement which helped me finish this dissertation. My special thanks go to Jody Mellor, Sanja Bilič, Zahra Tizro, and Cirihn Malpocher for sharing their research ideas and participating in intellectual debates. I have enjoyed every moment that we have worked together in reading groups and at workshops, seminars and conferences. I will always be grateful for your being there for me when I needed food for thought and emotional support.

I am grateful to the British Women Graduates' Foundation for financial support throughout the third year of my PhD study, as well as the British Sociological Association for enabling me to present at international conferences.

Finally, I would like to thank my sister Krysia, my parents Małgorzata and Henryk, and grandparents Bronisława and Henryk. I would not have achieved all this without your unconditional love and support. I am also greatly thankful to my husband Joe for his unwavering love, as well as insightful comments and tireless proofreading of my chapters, looking after me and keeping me going for this last, most fruitful, but also most difficult year.

Introduction

Technological developments over the past two decades have transformed the way in which people interact with each other and go about their daily business. The expansion of the Internet has even affected the way some people practise and experience religion. There are now for example religious social networks, such as *GodTube*, which was the fastest growing site in August 2007 (Eldon 2007). There are also specialized networks for Christians, Muslims, and Hindus.[1] Believers can also sign up to dating portals which allow them to label themselves as religious. But does technology reach beyond the mundane sphere of religion, into exegesis and the spiritual?

An important question is: to what extent does the combination of technology and religion duplicate existing debates, or transform them? Marshall McLuhan famously argued that 'the medium is the message' in his book *Understanding Media: The Extensions of Man* (1987). He believed that the medium permeated the message and remained in a symbiotic relationship with it. In other words, he claimed that information was shaped and conditioned by technology used to transmit it. Although McLuhan's concepts were widely critiqued and challenged as technological determinism (Baudrillard 1967; Williams 1975), it has been argued that the Internet assumes a certain degree of independence and 'plays' with the old triad 'message-medium-receiver', sometimes putting it in altogether new configurations (Morris and Ogan 1996). If the nature of the medium were to affect the message, how would Islam become different by being situated online?

Islam has a strong presence online, and its multiple interpretations have found their way into cyberspace (Anderson 1999, 2002; Bunt 2000, 2003, 2009). Muslims looking for scholars' opinions, translations and interpretations of the holy texts and debate go online to find the answers. The Internet provides both publishing opportunities and a wide audience, which, many authors have argued, has resulted in a gradual fragmentation of religious authority as the numbers of 'new interpreters' of Islam grow (Anderson 1999).

The presence of Muslim women on the Internet is rapidly increasing, yet their use of the Internet remains very under-researched. Muslim women who use this medium do so for a range of purposes, and this book is an exploration of one of these activities: discussing Islamic issues and interpreting Islamic texts in women-only Internet newsgroups (also known as discussion lists). It is a contribution to the debate on gender in Islam as expressed by the women themselves. In addition, it attempts to answer the question whether the location of these discussions on the Internet has implications for both Muslim women users and the wider debate on Islam.

There are Muslim women who argue that God has given them the right to not only learn about the religion, but also interpret its sources and dispute other interpretations (Afshar 2008). They believe that since the death of the Prophet Muhammad, who was a supporter and defender of women, their Islamic rights have been unlawfully claimed by men. These Muslim women see the source of this subordination embedded in the patriarchal social systems which deprive them of their God-given Islamic rights. They counter this by engaging directly with two Islamic sources: the *Qur'an*[2] (the holy book of Islam) and the *Ahadith* (also known as the traditions of the Prophet) (Barlas 2006). By constructing their own understandings of these texts, not only do they get closer to the core of Islam, they recover the knowledge of their rights and entitlements as well. As a consequence, many are interested in the transformation of the religious *status quo*, as they are often underprivileged in the current power dynamics.

At the same time, Muslim women are the centre of attention in two prominent discourses which have also been used to control them. In the discourse of Orientalism, they have been represented as silent, backward, and subjugated, because of Islam and 'oppressive' Muslim men (Ahmed 1992). This has subsequently made them vulnerable to the stereotype whereby they need to be rescued by white men. In her analysis of the situation in Afghanistan, Bickel writes: 'Powerful classic messages of strong good men defeating powerful evil are at work; Grimm's fairytales may have provided the story lines and protagonists for these would-be modern heroes, and Afghanistan was not the first time that the U.S. government positioned itself as the champion of women as part of a justification for military intervention' (2003: np). Although none of these representations of Muslim women as weak and oppressed are ahistorical and they are all products of specific 'moments and developments in culture', Muslim women today, especially those wearing the hijab, are still frequently perceived as stuck in the past, unable to cope with the challenges of the 'modern', western world (Bullock 2002: 67). They are also perceived as women without an agenda, unanimously accepting patriarchal social relations. In his Introduction to Ayaan Hirsi Ali's recent autobiographical novel *Infidel*, Christopher Hitchens, an American journalist supporting the invasion of Iraq, states (2008: xiv): 'The cause of backwardness and misery in the Muslim world is not Western oppression but Islam itself'. His writing, in which he argues that Muslim women will never be free and empowered unless they reject Islam, embodies the stereotype of deeply prejudiced Orientalism (see Said 1979). The recently emerging discourse focusing on the 'female Muslim terrorist'[3] is a variation of this Islamophobic attitude, as it insists that Muslim women are manipulated into carrying out suicide bombings (Chulov 2008; Hussein and McElroy 2008).

The patriarchal, conservative Islamist discourse also tends to essentialize women, although in a different way. The Islamic Revolution in Iran is an example of how successful political mobilization of women has resulted in creation by the state of a very rigid category of a human being, which results in women having fewer choices and being unable to perform all the existing roles in a society because of their gender (Afshar 1996). Official Islamist discourse tends to compare the western woman, who is constantly expected to play the role of a 'sex object' in the male-dominated world with the Muslim woman, who holds a much higher, respected position in her society and who enjoys many more rights, granted her by Islam (Afshar 1998). At the same time, Muslim women's position is formulated in static terms (emotional, irrational and passive) and their rights to make choices are limited (Afshar 1993; Hassan 2001; Bhimji 2005).

Both of these discourses, Orientalist and conservative, try to deny women their public agenda and voice, attempting to confine them to the privacy of their homes, where they can be more easily controlled. Examining Muslim women's voice that can be heard in public may help understand the lives of Muslim women and remove the imbalance which exists in the representations of their experience. The fact that 'ordinary', non-academic Muslim women discuss Islam online indicates that an independent quest for knowledge has become a common way of obtaining an Islamic education. Such theological quests have the potential to shape women's identities; women are able to access and discuss Islamic knowledge and, subsequently, apply their own interpretations of this knowledge to their own actions. This shapes their perceptions of who they are online and offline. In the newsgroups they construct their identities through their narratives of their epistemological and hermeneutical positions; in the offline world they develop their identities through choices and actions based on their positions (Karam 1998). Hence the second part of the book title, *Faith and Identity in the Virtual World*. Muslim women's faith-based identities, no matter how diverse, are the focus of this book. Other aspects of identities, related to ethnicity, age, location and language, although also significant and undoubtedly affecting women's understandings of their selves, remain almost completely concealed. This is due to the specificity of the research setting, women's only discussion groups where most women remain anonymous.

This book has two key aims. First, it examines the nature and potential implications of these intellectual online debates, which, like their participants, have not received much public attention, and second, it considers the stereotype, reinforced by the non-Muslim media and still prominent, that Muslim women are submissive and voiceless because of Islam and its values (Afshar 2008). The book explores how these women engage with Islamic sources and exegesis; how they interact with each other and how this interaction impacts their meaning making. The fact that these processes are occurring on the Internet and in English, adds an important dimension which needs to be considered. Who are the Muslim women who use technology to argue their point in Islamic discussions? How willing are they to accept the generalizing constructions of their identities as conceptualized by modern Orientalist and Islamist discourses? Does the fact that they discuss Islam online and in English, the *lingua franca* of the contemporary world, have any serious implications for the findings?

Methodology

The newsgroups which provided the data for analysis were populated by Muslim women (and a few non-Muslim women interested in Islam) of different ages, nationalities, and ethnicities. They did not congregate on the basis of these characteristics; the quality that formed the basis of their membership was *being Muslim*. This was conveyed by members' narratives, for example in new members' introductory postings which began with declarations that they were Muslim. Being Muslim was reflected by newsgroup names that always included the terms 'Muslim', 'Islam', or 'believers'.

It seems pertinent that here I consider terminology used throughout the book. It is argued that a lack of subtlety (or indeed, crudeness) in the use of the term has reflected the Orientalist tendency to homogenize and control (Bullock 2002). Just like the veil is deployed today as the signifier of Muslimness (without the consideration that there are non-Muslim women who veil, or that there are Muslim women who do not veil), the term 'Muslim woman' triggers specific associations such as submission, silence, servitude, lack of agency (Khan 2000). It also prevents a discussion of differences between women across the world (whether related to ethnicity, nationality, culture, age, socioeconomic status or body ability) who share the characteristic of being Muslim. The author cooke (2007) has coined a neologism, 'Muslimwoman', that reflects this act of lumping together and depriving of individuality. In cooke's understanding 'Muslimwoman' is constructed to invoke a singular identification, it is ascribed to those who may not necessarily identify with the imaginary that is attached to it. Aware of the neo-Orientalist and patriarchal Islamic discourses that tend to essentialize the 'Muslim woman' as a fixed, homogenous creature inhabiting both Muslim-majority and Muslim-minority contexts (Khan 2002), I nevertheless acknowledge that some women may choose to select being Muslim as their key identity, which Spivak (1987) calls 'strategic essentialism'. It is important that it is the individuals themselves who prioritize the chosen identity and that it is not enforced by others; strategic essentialism allows a collective identity and creating political links. Castells (2004) points to the role of media in the formation of identities by arguing that alliances organized around a primary identity have been intensified by the emergence of global information technologies. Similarly, cooke (2007: 141) notes that 'new media produce radical connectivity across the globe and foster a new kind of cosmopolitanism marked by religion'. Echoeing Spivak, she notes that certain identifications can be strategically deployed, however, they must be open to deconstruction and contestations from within. Strategic adopting of the identity 'Muslim woman' was the case with all the researched newsgroups, which were very diverse and attracted women from many walks of life. Therefore, I use the category 'Muslim women' throughout the book, as I believe it is my duty as a feminist researcher

(Clare and Hamilton 2003) to honour the participants' self-definitions and to talk about them using the label they identify with.

The literature I discuss sometimes focuses on a sub-category of the category Muslim; it may acknowledge either women's ethnicity, or geographic location. I am careful not to confuse these terms as some religious practices and online behaviours are bound to be different in many ways for each of these groups. However, I have decided to tease out the findings which might apply to Muslim women of different ethnic and national origins; therefore I use the term 'Muslim women' also when I indend to point out that a certain statement is not likely to be limited to just one group but can be used in a more general sense.

Most members of the newsgroups seemed to be located in the United States, and possible implications of this fact are considered in Chapter 6. Many of them were converts to Islam, but there were also American Muslims of Arabic, Turkish, Indian, Pakistani, and Indonesian descent. There were also British, Finnish, Canadian, Romanian, and German Muslims as well as women from Muslim majority countries, such as Saudi Arabia, Iran and Indonesia. The diversity of the members was also reflected by their occupations, which varied from engineers, graphic designers, nurses, teachers, shop assistants and receptionists to stay-at-home mothers. They followed various brands of Islam: Sunni (including the four schools of thought), Salafi, Shi'a, or 'just Islam'. However, only a small number of women chose to discuss their lives and identities in detail, with a majority focusing on discussing Islamic perspectives on a range of issues. Unfortunately, newsgroups do not collect or provide statistics in regard to nationality or ethnicity of their members, so I can only provide an approximation of demographic data based on my observations.

The absence of other information about the participants further emphasises the importance of the primary identity that they share and their aim – to increase gendered Islamic knowledge. Castells (2004: 195) captures this spirit of a knowledge-based network when he argues:

> The fourth element inducing the challenge to patriarchalism is the rapid diffusion of ideas in a globalized culture, and in an interrelated world, where people and experience travel and mingle, quickly weaving a hyperquilt of women's voices throughout most of the planet.

The newsgroups discussed in this book may indeed be the first forum where Muslim women from all walks of life across the globe can come together as an almost anonymous collective weaving a hyperquilt consisting of diverse interpretations of Islamic texts and issues faced by the participants in their localised contexts.

The newsgroups that I accessed are located on an American server. Technically speaking, they are e-mail groups, where all members can read and respond to each other's contributions. Although they range in size from 500 to 5,000 members, it is difficult to assess the numbers of active contributors and lurkers. This proportion has an impact on group dynamics, as the number of active members is related to the number of contributions that keep the group alive. All the newsgroups share a number of characteristics, such as an emphasis on their Islamic identity through displaying Islamic imagery and the use of Islamic vocabulary on their public homepage. They all inform their visitors that their goal is to promote Islam and further their personal knowledge of it. They invite all women to join (including non-Muslims, as long as they respect the rules and do not disrupt the group). All new members receive special guidelines, for instance, that expressing Islamophobic views may result in removal from the group. Members are asked to refrain from expressing hate and slandering. There is a great emphasis on the importance of sisterhood and the *Ummah*, which is reflected in the groups' names: the most commonly used signifiers are 'sisters', 'women', 'Muslim' and 'Islamic'.

The demographic structure of the groups is unknown; all that is required to join is an email account which can be set up anonymously, and members are not expected to disclose any personal details to their groups. However, it seems from the postings where women refer to their geographical location, that many are located in the United States. This was confirmed by a poll in one of the groups (on a non-representative number of participants). The rest are scattered around the world, with a prominent presence of contributors from the Middle East and South Asia. Factors such as age are also impossible to assess. Many contributors are students and mothers of young children, and there is also a visible group of women in their 40s and 50s.

The groups claim to be women-only; men are asked to refrain from joining, yet one cannot be certain that all contributors are female due to the degree of anonymity on the Internet. There are techniques to assess honesty of Internet users in that respect (Donath 1999) and so the newsgroup moderators may assess the applications of potential members who are likely to have online profiles elsewhere to confirm the gender of an individual. Furthermore, it is argued that the lack of visual cues provokes self-disclosure (Caspi and Gorsky 2006); therefore, an impostor is likely to reveal enough information to be uncovered. Finally, there is evidence that gender deception is most likely to happen in online groups where sex is the main topic of conversation (Turkle 1995), with a considerably lower degree of deception in other online contexts (Donath 1998). Also, gender is the factor that is misrepresented considerably less frequently than, for example age, occupation, income and education (Caspi and Gorsky 2006). However, this data refers to mixed-gender online environments where gender is not a criterion for inclusion. I assume that because being a woman is critical to gaining access to the Muslim women's newsgroups, the level of deception may be initially higher, but moderators scrutinize the applicants more closely for the very same reason, for example, potential members' online profiles are screened in order to establish their gender.

All communications with participants – group members and moderators – were conducted via email and newsgroup boards. Nine women initiated e-mail exchanges with me, offering to share their experiences. Data used in the research encompassed postings sent to the newsgroups between 2001 and 2006. Their contents determined the structure of this book, which is organized according to the themes which very clearly emerged from the online discussions. The overarching theme was the shape of gender relations in Islam – discussed from many perspectives: contemporary and historical; theoretical and as 'lived experience'; finally, as interpreted by progressive and conservative scholars. The issue of gender relations in Islam became a framework for women's discussion of other subjects, and was never absent from their analyses.

As this research focuses on individual, personal understandings of Islam, voices of women are central to the analysis. Through women's online discussions, we have the opportunity to obtain knowledge on issues they deem significant and to learn how women analyse and link them with Islam. Therefore, inclusion of feminist perspectives in my methodology was dictated by my focus on women's experiences (Ramazanoğlu and Holland 2002). Although, as it is often pointed out, there are no methodologies or methods that are in exclusive use by feminist researchers (Harding 1987; Brayton 1997; Ramazanoğlu and Holland 2002), certain motives, concerns and knowledge brought into the research project can make it uniquely feminist (Brayton 1997). Importantly, knowledge produced by a feminist project can be useful for transformation of 'gendered injustice and subordination' (Ramazanoğlu and Holland 2002: 147) because feminist researchers are accountable to a community of women; their research is for women, and is grounded in women's experiences. It acknowledges the importance of accounts of life in unjust gendered relationships (Ramazanoğlu and Holland 2002).

My choice of methods, non-participant observation and textual analysis, was a result of the feminist belief in the need to listen to women's voices. I read Muslim women's newsgroup archives and observed the ongoing discussions in order to 'let the women speak'. I did not approach the data with prescribed categories or structure of the analysis in mind. Due to this, I ensured that the research, and in particular, data analysis, was conducted on the participants' terms as far as possible; all the categories used while discussing the data emerged from the women's own discussions.

A feminist researcher has to allow the participant to speak so that the account of her experience remains as accurate as possible; the power dynamics which may emerge during the course of the research are taken into account. It must be ensured that the research is conducted ethically by anonymizing the data (unless participants wish otherwise), obtaining informed consent where possible, acting in a respectful and open manner, as well as explaining to the participants the aim and method of the research, so that they are fully informed about it, and subsequently, sharing the findings with them. A feminist researcher carefully thinks about her own positionality in the research process and assesses the potential risks which it may carry.

My position in this research is that of a relative outsider. I am a non-Muslim woman, but I do not have a typical 'western' cultural and academic background. Coming from Eastern Europe I initially found the western traditions and debates foreign, and I did not carry the historic baggage of colonial conquests and 'privileged', white, middle-class feminism. I believe that there are different kinds of 'whiteness' which might be theorized in the categories 'western' and 'eastern white', and that they carry very different implications for their representatives. Thus, I argue that I am 'other' in the West, both in academic and non-academic environments, a quality I share with these participants in this study who live in the West. My perceived 'otherness', however, does not wipe out the differences between me and the participants. They are Muslim but I am not, and the dynamic between us would have probably been different if I were. However, the participants welcomed me very kindly as a newsgroup member and, after initial 'testing' of my views they were glad that a non-Muslim scholar wanted to contribute to research on Islam. My ethnicity did not seem to play an important part during my short interaction with the participants, and I was asked about the origins of my interest in Islam rather than my ethnic background. However, I was always aware that my positionality as a white, non-Muslim woman working at a western university influenced the way I looked at the data and analysed it.

As a Polish feminist with a strong interest in Islam developed during my research visit to Turkey in 2003 I was interested in discussions where Islamic perspectives on gender were developed and reshaped. I wanted to learn what the grassroots Muslim women, without a public profile and not engaged in exclusively academic or activist pursuits, thought about the status that Islam gave women, and how their lived experience as believing women has transformed over the years. These newsgroups seemed a perfect place for this study, as they bring together women who explore, learn and interpret the Qur'an and other Islamic texts in order to reveal their meaning.

Non-participant observation of the newsgroups gave me the advantage of being able to observe past and ongoing interaction in its natural setting as all the posts were archived. I accessed the conversations in their original form, and I was not constrained by time, place and context of data generation. On the contrary, I could select any online discussions that happened after 2001, therefore was able to discern trends in a relatively large corpus of data. Non-observant participation also offered the advantage of reading and analysing the original data at my own pace, as opposed to the interview method, which allows the researcher to interact freely only with interview transcripts. While non-participant observation in a traditional setting is commonly associated with covert research (which is ethically controversial), I was able to observe past interactions and avoid unethical conduct by requesting consent from participants who I could still contact through email.

Eventually I decided to use the data produced before I joined the groups. This was useful in prioritizing the participants' voices in the research in the sense that at the time the writings were produced, there was no researcher in the groups, therefore the women were not inhibited in expressing their views, or did not feel they were expected to say certain things as, for example, Mellor (2007) reports her participants did. She writes that her participants feel a sense of obligation to talk about issues they felt the researcher would be most interested in. My interest in issues exactly as raised by the participants themselves prevented me from conducting follow-up email interviews with group members, despite claims that interpretation of observation has to be 'confirmed' by further interrogation of the participants (Lincoln and Guba 1985). Furthermore, such claims imply that there is 'one, objective, and knowable social reality', a statement that many qualitative researchers would contradict (Mason 2002: 190). Employing an additional data production method (to carry out triangulation) would indeed provide me with more, different data that could enrich this project.

The decision to use data which was produced before I started the research has given the research a document analysis slant. The data was in the form of textually recorded online discussions. The closest parallel I could think of was historical research on the contents of letter exchanges. However, the research on online discussions entailed other things absent in the research on letters – the large number of authors, and perhaps more importantly, the sense of community. The postings included references not only to the author and immediate partners in the interactions, but more often than not, they addressed the entire group. In that sense, the method had to anticipate some elements of interaction analysis. This is a useful, interdisciplinary analysis method for the empirical investigation of interaction between human beings. Such interaction may involve talk, non-verbal interaction, and the use of artefacts and technologies (Jordan and Henderson 1995). The epistemological assumption that underpins interaction analysis is that knowledge and action are 'fundamentally social in origin, organisation, and use, and are situated in particular social and material ecologies' (Jordan and Henderson 1995: 41). One of the points that interaction analysis raises is 'how people make sense of each other's actions as meaningful and orderly' (Jordan and Henderson 1995: 41). This is also a consideration that underpins this research project, to a certain extent, as it takes this issue further and investigates how Muslim women express their understandings of each other's words.

In this research it would be difficult to establish the shape of power relations between the author and the participants. Whereas the positionality of the researcher can be easily revealed (late 20s, white, Polish, 'culturally Catholic'; heterosexual, middle-class, able-bodied), it is assumed that participants are a heterogeneous group (different ages, races, nationalities, sexualities, class backgrounds, levels of able-bodiedness). Some of these factors are hardly mentioned in the newsgroups, but their invisibility to the researcher's eyes does not mean that they are not at play. It is assumed in the newsgroups that the factor which unites the participants is the religion of Islam (there are non-Muslim newsgroup members, but they tend to make it known in their postings). Therefore, the known difference between me and the participants is religious. A lack of a researcher's appropriate knowledge about Islam and Muslims could lead to homogenization and objectification of the participants. It is agreed that a researcher brings to the research not only her social position, education and skills but also ignorance and limitations (Gorelick 1991). To remedy this, I attended courses on Islamic history and contemporary Islam. I also had in-depth conversations with Muslim women in the areas of York and London (not the newsgroup members) to gain a deeper understanding of the diversity of women who regard Islam as their religion. However, I was careful that my interest in Islam and sympathy for participants should not take the shape of patronizing (McRobbie 1982), 'pseudo-scientific' interest, 'fetishizing' (Boyd 2009: 29) or false intimacy.

Working with anti- or non-feminist women may constitute a problem for a feminist researcher – or being a feminist researcher can be problematic when working with anti- or non-feminist women. Women in the newsgroups discussed the pros and cons of feminism and I inevitably I found myself drawn to the postings of those who expressed their sympathy or stated that they were feminists. Indeed, faced with anti-feminist views expressed by some women, I initially did not know what to make of them. Whereas it is possible for some anti-feminist women and feminists to agree on certain points, such as the harmfulness of pornography (Luff 1999), researchers describe a similar feeling of uneasiness upon realising that their participants' views may be diametrically different from their own (Herman 1994). My attention was focused on those women who I could identify with, and when I was reading and interpreting their writings, I did not experience any discomfort. However, I later realized that my sense of familiarity with views of only some of the participants might lead to silencing of others. This was a 'cold shower' for me, and made me go back to the data and look at it from a new perspective. I recognized that engaging with women's voices meant including all of them in the final picture. I was also aware that my analysis of anti-feminist women's postings must be very careful as I would likely be less sympathetic to their views, and therefore, may dismiss them or subconsciously treat them as less important.

There is no one ethical code for Internet researchers, but there are general guidelines suggested by the Association of Internet Researchers

(Ess and Jones 2004). Among others, it advocates considering the character of the research context (visible (public) or invisible (private), who the posters are (children or adults, vulnerable individuals), what harm the research could result in, what makes consent truly informed and the use the data will later be put to. There is growing acknowledgement of the importance of sensitivity and reflectivity in research, as in the past many studies of online contexts failed to make proper ethical considerations (Thomas 2004). There is also an emerging body of work on feminist online ethics. Olivero and Lunt (2004) have developed a feminist ethics model in e-mail interviewing, where they emphasize the importance of rapport between the researcher and participant. Such a relationship, based on equal participation and trust, is supported by the relaxed, asynchronous interviewing mode, where the presence of researcher and immediacy of response do not constraint the participant, offering 'prototypical conditions for a negotiated, as well as reflexive, construction of meaning' (Olivero and Lunt 2004: 107). They conclude that feminist ethics and e-mail interviewing are particularly harmonious. This suggests that the method I used in this research, non-participant online observation, may also have potential from the feminist ethics viewpoint, as it is similarly asynchronous. However, discussions of ethics in online contexts are focused on general research guidelines or more specifically, the interviewing method (Johns *et al.* 2004; Mann and Stewart 2000; Dolowitz *et al.* 2008; Fielding *et al.* 2008) and to date, few feminist ethical guidelines or models in relation to observations have been developed – the book edited by Markham and Baym (2009) is a notable exception.

The main ethical consideration in the data production stage of my research was to properly inform newsgroup members who I was and what I hoped to do, with their help. To achieve this, I sent out an introductory posting to the group describing myself, my planned research and my motivations to do it. I repeatedly posted information about my presence in the group and requested a reaction in case it was unwelcome. I never experienced a negative reaction, but women did ask me to disclose some of my earlier writings so that they knew my views on Islam. They explained that as long as my intention was not 'slandering Islam' in my dissertation, they felt happy to share their thoughts with me. They presented it as their mission to 'dispel myths about Islam among non-Muslims'. However, they requested full confidentiality, which is also an ethical requirement in research online (Dolowitz *et al.* 2008). I pledged to use pseudonyms or codes in my analysis to prevent women from being identified. In this respect, the fact that the newsgroups are password-protected, prevents the contents of the archive from leaking out to the general public. For example they cannot be 'googled', and it would be impossible to make a connection between a quote in my dissertation and its author. This is a prerequisite to protect the participants from harm, which loss of anonymity would constitute. Offline contexts of the research were not known to me; some women might have been accessing and posting in secret, therefore it was crucial to maximize their anonymity in my research. King (1996) lists actions necessary to properly anonymize a posting from a private group removing all headers and signatures; references to a person's name or pseudonym within the citation; references to the name and type of the group; references to the location of the group (if applicable); and storing the data in a secure manner.

As Blank writes, 'there is no "free lunch" in online data collection' (2008: 541). Although access to participants is relatively low-cost and time effective, it entails a set of complex and ethically difficult issues. Anonymity of participants, the first condition of online ethics, may be compromised by the loss of transcripts, which are in the form of text files. Confidentiality must be accompanied by asking for informed consent of all participants whose writings are to be quoted in the analysis (although some researchers argue that if information was posted to a publicly accessible group, it is already in public domain and informed consent is not necessary; Fahy 2007). Applying the feminist understanding of ownership of words, I asked for permission to use people's writings, indicating exactly which part of which posting I hoped to use and why (e.g. to illustrate an argument, or to show a variety of opinions). By asking for consent, I gave them the chance to refuse at that point and also later, if they wished to do so. In an online context, ensuring that the participants are fully informed is more problematic than in a face-to-face context, as the contact with the researcher is limited, but on the other hand, it is argued that participants do not feel pressured in online research situations, as they can refuse more freely, and paradoxically, they are more likely to consent to participation in the research (Eynon *et al.* 2008). It is pointed out that a request for informed consent must be formulated in a clear and straightforward manner (Eynon *et al.* 2008). A researcher must be ready to answer questions, explain her research to potential participants, and make sure that her explanations are understood. There are specific techniques to ensure the understanding of the participants, including quizzes, although they present a dilemma whereby the researcher may monopolize participants' time and increase a risk of dropout (Varnhagen *et al.* 2005). In my contact with participants, when asking for consent, I expected brief 'yes' or 'no' responses and did not envisage much communication, exactly for the fear of 'stealing women's time'. However, women reacted with much more interest and curiosity than I anticipated – they asked me a lot of questions about my life and my research, which was in common with the way Giacaman's (1988) research proceeded.

'Unethical feminist research' is an oxymoron. An ethical and sensitive approach is integral to feminist perspectives as feminist researchers rejected the dogmas of 'objective and scientific research', such as indifference towards the researched (Gorelick 1991: 461), and instead produced a set of methodological guidelines that advocated 'conscientization' of both the researcher and the researched (Mies 1983). Maintaining ethical standards is also helpful to other researchers – Internet users subjected to covert research are likely to later refuse permission to all researchers, even to those who intend to undertake their study in a sensitive and ethical way (Barnes 2004).

The power of language and voice

All newsgroup discussions were held in English, which at first glance may not seem surprising as roughly half of the members live in the United States. It is uncertain though, how many members speak English as their first language. A considerable number of the US-based women are migrants, so it can be assumed that their native languages are other than English. What does it mean that Muslim women in the newsgroups use English to discuss Islam? Who is included and who is excluded in these discussions? How does the use of English influence the discussions? Other exclusion factors, such as age, education, and socioeconomic status must also be considered.

There are a number of issues that reflect the uneasiness of the relationship between Islam and English; British colonization of Muslim territories in the past; the fact that the current occupant armies in Iraq and Afghanistan are mainly Anglophone (Karmani 2005); the fact that English has been a carrier of Judeo-Christian values and used for missionary purposes (Makoni and Pennycook 2005; Mohd-Asraf 2005); and the fact that English is an exclusion factor in the developing world, where a gap exists between the English educated and non-English educated, with the former belonging to the socioeconomic elite, and the latter representing the non-elite (Mohd-Asraf 2005). Despite these concerns, in the current *status quo*, English seems to have gained popularity as the online language of Muslim users. Arabic, the language which has a special status in Islam because it is the language in which the Qur'an was revealed, is spoken by 280 million native speakers and 250 million non-native speakers, whereas it was estimated as early as 1985 that English was spoken by one and a half billion speakers (native and non-native) (Alptekin 2002). Islam is a majority religion in 57 countries, with Indonesia being the most populous. Islam is also the second religion in a number of countries, such as the United Kingdom and France. There are American Muslims, for whom English is the first or second language (there is no accurate count of American Muslims — numbers vary from 1.1 to 7 million). In 1990 there were between 12 and 15 million European Muslims who spoke European languages (Ramadan 1999). The cultural diversity within Islam is related to linguistic diversity; in this situation, English has become a language through which many Muslims choose to communicate online with other Muslims, including about Islamic matters. The use of English in online presentations of Islam may increase Islam's potential influence on non-Muslims.

Some of the participants in my research project report that their first contact with Islam happened online, during casual browsing of websites. Van Nieuwkerk (2006) reports the case of a woman who converted on the internet, taking the *shahada*[4] in English in the presence of two women who were chatting to her at that moment. It can be argued that English has been appropriated by Muslims, who are bound by religion but differ in cultural and linguistic terms. This appropriation does not mean that Arabic (or other languages, for that matter) are out of use in the Muslim online realm. A study by Palfreyman and al-Khalil (2003) evidences that ASCII-ised Arabic (Arabic that can be written down in the Latin alphabet) is commonly used by female university students from the United Arab Emirates in instant messaging. An exploration of women's online discussions in Arabic, Persian and other languages would certainly contribute to the understanding of global Muslim women's voices.

All included quotes from participants' postings are in their original form, and I have maintained all typos and emphases, with a few exceptions where I specifically mentioned that emphasis was mine. Preserving the original form of the data, with its typographical errors, was a conscious decision, as I agree with Markham (2004: 153) that rewriting participants' contributions may be ethically problematic. Markham writes:

> We literally reconfigure these people [participants] when we edit their sentences, because for many of them, these messages are a deliberate presentation of self. Even when they are not deliberate, texts construct the essence and meaning of the participant, as perceived and responded to by others.

The living language of the transcripts emphasizes the dynamic and performative aspect of online interactions (Mann and Stewart 2000). Original text produced by participants is significant, because in online contexts embodiment is constructed with the means of text, in contrast to traditonal research where embodied situations are observed, possibly recorded, and written up later. This text may be the only means through which participants know and react to each other; therefore, it has to be preserved.

Given the relative absence of Muslim women's expressions in the mainstream western media, the Internet is a useful space to research the increasingly visible links between Muslim women's faith, identities and voices. As Tayyibah Taylor, publisher and editor-in-chief of *Azizah*, a magazine produced by and for Muslim women, said in her speech at an event organized by the Muslim Women's League of America (2003: np):

> Now, more than ever, we need our own media. At a time when the expression of dissenting views is deemed unpatriotic, and objective journalism seems to be out of vogue, we need our own media. This is also a time in journalism when ratings and the bottom line are more important than content and when the media sources are merging to become mega-outlets in the hands of a few. We need our own outlets to ensure our voice is heard.

The Azizah magazine is one such outlet that brings Muslim women's voices and concerns to the fore and acts as a platform for the exchange of their views. The Internet has enabled the emergence of Muslim women's newsgroups which have a similar function to Azizah and, like Azizah, are Muslim women's own independent media and spaces.

Notes

1   For example, http://www.xianz.com/, http://www.muslimsocial.com/, http://www.allindians.com/, all accessed on 22 July 2009.
2   Non-English terms used in this book appear in italics only at first occurrence, as recommended by the *Chicago Manual of Style* (2010).
3   Since 9/11 there has been a proliferation of work on Islam, whose authors address the terrorist attacks in New York and Washington as a turning point in the study of Muslims in the West (e.g. Edmunds and Turner 2005). This was also signified by the title of a conference organised by the University of Oxford in 2003: 'Muslims in Europe, post 9/11: Understanding and Responding to the Islamic World'. In my view, this approach draws attention away from the discrimination of Muslims and other challenges, such as the stereotyping of Muslim women, which they faced long before 9/11 (Weller *et al.* 2001; Ahmed 1992).
4   The Islamic declaration of faith.

1 Islamic feminisms?

The key question in this book is how the use of the Internet facilitates Muslim women's religious dialogues. In this chapter I assess a range of literature relevant to Muslim women's online voices, activities and experiences; this includes work about their identities, as well as their various understandings of Islam and relationship with technology. One key theme that arises is the question of Islamic feminism. Although it is a category considered unwieldy by many authors and activists, its exploration is helpful in understanding Muslim women's struggles for the recognition of their rights. An exploration of current academic debates on gender justice and equality held by Muslim women allows a better understanding of their activities on the Internet today.

Although in 2011 Muslim women are by no means a new category of Internet user, there is little existing research focusing on their online activities. The bulk of the available literature on religious online communities has not addressed the possibility that there may be something specific about this group and its online experiences. However, there is an extensive body of literature on the relationship between religion and technology. The researched contexts include online Islamic environments; online religious communities; women's spiritual online groups. I investigate these areas in order to understand the whole context of Muslim women's online communications; their online groups exist as a part of wider trends that have emerged on the Internet.

Islamic feminism(s)

Muslim women's online discussions have not emerged in a vacuum – I argue that they are a very modern extension of an intellectual debate which commenced a long time ago, although neither the exact time of its beginning nor its name is agreed on. According to academics such as Afshar (1993), cooke (2002) and Armstrong (2006) the debate on the status of women in Islam and Muslim societies began in the times of the Prophet Muhammad, when women joined him in his mission to spread Islam on equal terms with men; alternately, others, such as Badran (1996) argue for a more recent origin, in the zenith of western colonialism which occurred in the 19th century. The name that is now often used to describe this debate, Islamic feminism, is controversial, as it is not accepted by all campaigners for Muslim women's empowerment. Some refuse to carry this label – even if their work can be interpreted by others as an articulation of feminism (Göle 1996; Barlas 2004).

Apart from Islamic feminism, there is a rich literature on 'Muslim' and 'secular' Middle Eastern feminism. Whereas Muslim feminists accept engagement with non-Muslim feminism and its values, their framework remains Islamic and, together with most Islamic feminists, they argue that an antipatriarchal reinterpretation of Islamic sources is necessary (Karam 1998). In contrast, for secular feminists living in Muslim-majority countries, Islam is nothing more than a state religion and law (Moghissi 1999). They argue that de-Islamization is necessary in order to achieve women's empowerment (Azad, in Moghissi 1998) and further claim that Islamic feminism is an oxymoron due to the hostility against feminist values that is inherent in Islamic laws (Tohidi 2003). Historically, secular feminists were connected with international feminism and with national independence struggles (Badran 2001a).

There is no consistency in the use of the categories 'Muslim', 'Islamic' and 'secular' as descriptors of feminism. For example, Tohidi (2003) uses 'Muslim' and 'Islamic' feminisms as synonyms, whereas Moghissi (1999: 134) discusses both Islamic and secular feminisms under the heading of 'Muslim feminism', because she understands the term 'Muslim' as 'originating from a Muslim state'. Barlas (2004) refers to the secularist position as 'Muslim feminism'[1] and contrasts it with 'Islamic feminism'.

Karam (1998) addresses three types of feminism: secular, Muslim and Islamist. Unlike Barlas, she differentiates between secular feminists (who articulate their feminism outside of the religious discourse) and Muslim feminists (who argue for gender equality, call for re-reading and re-evaluation of the Islamic sources, and sometimes reject the weak[2] Ahadith, which they consider misogynist). Her third category are Islamist feminists who reject the western debates on the equality of the genders and work within an Islamic framework which they consider as not requiring re-reading or re-interpreting. Karam's justification for using the term 'feminist' to refer to women who might reject it is that a difference must be made between Islamists whose work is parallel to that of feminists outside of the Islamic world and explicitly non-feminist Islamists whose views are in opposition to the discourse of gender equality/justice. Islamic feminists call for recognition of 'gender complementarity', a concept which is based on the belief that gender differences are constructed naturally and socially, and that men and women's roles are complementary and together constitute a totality (Rahman 1980).

Karam insists that the three types of feminism are not separate positions; on the contrary, she argues that they are all in 'a state of flux, and are context- and issue bound rather than clear-cut and immutable' (1998: 9). It is therefore more pertinent to analyse the positions as being part of one continuum. In this book I do not address the secularist position, which rejects Islam completely, as I focus on women's religious discourses.

Some women interested in the question of women's status in Islam refuse to be labelled as 'Islamic feminists' due to the perceived negative connotations of the term 'feminism'. These include a rejection of religion and traditional values, patronizing attitudes to women of other cultures, as well a focus on the problems of exclusively white, western, middle-class women. Abdelatif and Ottaway (2007) write that interviews with women activists in both Hizbollah and the Muslim Brotherhood reveal rejection of and contempt for the concept of western feminism, which they interpreted not as a struggle for the recognition of the rights of women, but as a movement to free women from all social constraints and obligations to family and community, leading to excessive individualism and even licentiousness. For these women activists, 'Islam and feminism are two contradictory terms', and they were not interested in discussing possible common goals that they and western feminists might have, although they set similar demands – a right to education, work, and political participation. They see Islamic feminism as equally unacceptable as western feminism because they believe that Islamic feminism is only a mutation of western feminism, covered with a thin mantle of Islam.

An alternative construct for the study of Muslim women's positions has been employed by Hafez (2003), who uses a more descriptive term – 'Islamic women's activism' – in her analysis of the self-empowerment of politically active women in Egypt. The decision against using the term 'feminism' not only removes the need to explain the binaries 'feminist/antifeminist' or 'Muslim/Islamic feminist' but, Hafez argues, enables her to remain in harmony with the way participants view their activities. The questions which occupy feminists of today, such as the veil or women's leadership, were not at all central to her participants' work, in which they strove to attain a proximity to God, which in turn allowed redefinition of their roles as women.

Badran (2001a) observes that distance between secular and religious women is constantly diminishing. She reports that secular women increasingly use religious discourse. According to Badran, the space between religious and secular positions is occupied by a new discourse, which she calls 'holistic feminism'. It is, to date, the least well articulated form of feminism and can be discerned in regions that have experienced little contact with European colonialism (e.g. in Yemen). Within it, the categories 'secular' or 'religious' have never been meaningful as it does not operate on the basis of a secular-religious binary. It is non-confrontational and accepts and consolidates women's struggle regardless of their hermeneutic position. To evidence this, Badran provides examples of feminist collaboration between women from different political and religious backgrounds in the Middle East.

Abdelatif and Ottaway (2007) observe that unlike Islamic activists, Muslim women academics do not reject the term 'Islamic feminism' outright, although they sharply delineate it from other feminisms. Accordingly, Barlas (2004) argues that for the term 'Islamic feminism' to acquire wider recognition, two distinctions must be made – between different types of feminism and between Islam and Muslims/Muslim practices. As long as, on the one hand, the realities of Muslims' lives are conflated with the teachings of Islam, and on the other hand, feminism is conflated with the radical strand of feminism which rejected the institutions of marriage, family and religion (see Echols 1989), a common understanding of women's struggle for rights cannot emerge.

It has to be noted that Islamic feminists' position is different from that of traditionalists, sometimes also referred to as Islamists'[3] who reject the claims of gender equality and believe that men are superior to women, who must focus on their duties as mothers and wives, preferably staying at home.[4] They argue that these priorities are a result of their special status which provides them with other responsibilities. Women's education and professional work are accepted as long as they do not conflict with the interest of family. Islamists argue that women are not created to function in leadership roles (Hijab 1988).

Kandiyoti (1987) argues that acceptance of male supremacy, whether forced or not, may be what she calls the 'patriarchal bargain' – a rational decision-making process in which women agree to some patriarchal practices in return for freedom of action in other areas. For instance, the women of Iran have accepted a gender-segregation policy and compulsory veiling but are allowed to attend university as long as they conform to the state's restrictions. Similarly, the right-wing women activists of Hizbollah and the Muslim Brotherhood, although absent from official candidate lists for the parliamentary elections, are able to run the women's branches of these organizations and push for change by opening up the debate on women's rights with the organizations' leaders (Abdelatif and Ottaway 2007).

In the most general terms, Islamic feminism can be described as an effort to reclaim women's rights which is based on Islamic sources. However, both the nature of women's Islamic rights and the validity of some Islamic sources are disputed.[5] The term 'Islamic feminism' depends on individual understanding of what constitutes Islamic sources and what rights these sources grant women. For instance, Badran (in Barlas 2004: 1, emphasis added) defines Islamic feminism as 'a discourse of gender equality and social justice that derives its understanding and mandate from the Qur'an and seeks *the practice* of rights and justice for *all* human beings in the totality of their existence across the public-private continuum', therefore defining the rights as gender equality and social justice, whilst taking the Qur'an as their source. This is a very broad definition as gender equality and social justice may be interpreted differently by different agents; it clearly excludes other Islamic sources, and this could be problematic from the point of view of mainstream Islam.

However, it can be argued that the lack of agreement on the scope and nature of Islamic feminism is advantageous, as a rigid definition would prevent further explorations of the theme. Whether the term 'Islamic feminism' is judged by individual authors as a useful category or a hindrance in their argument, its complexity indicates the need to consider carefully all the dimensions of Muslim women's backgrounds, views and strategies.

Reading Islamic sources in a liberation mode

The argument of Muslim and Islamic feminists is that the original, social justice-oriented meaning of the Qur'an has been obscured by exegesis serving the interests of males. They advocate women's close engagement with the Qur'an in order to challenge these patriarchal or misogynist interpretations. There are many works that discuss how this engagement ought to be exercised (Hassan 1988; Mernissi 1992; Wadud 1999 2000 and 2006; Barazangi 2004; Barlas 2006). All of them address the issue of new readings of the Qur'an, discussing the epistemological, ontological and methodological questions in their work that emerged in their own readings.

In this section I explore Hassan's writings, which draw attention to the Judeo-Christian influences on the patriarchal interpretations of Islamic sources and Barlas's methodology, which stresses the necessity of a holistic reading of Islamic sources. I also address Wadud's argument as to why re-reading of Islamic sources is necessary. A discussion of their perspectives is helpful in understanding the online discussions and readings of the Qur'an and Ahadith executed by Muslim women today, especially as academic Muslim women's engagement with Islamic texts preceeded, and to some extent shaped, much wider Muslim women's involvement in theological study.

Hassan's (1988) focus is on Islam's account of the creation of humankind. She deconstructs the story of Adam and Eve, the rib, and original sin, comparing the Islamic account with its Christian and Jewish counterparts. Her analysis stems from a careful study of the Qur'an and the Ahadith, especially the women-related passages, and the writings of Christian and Jewish feminist theologians who attempt to trace the origins of misogynist ideas in their traditions. She identifies three 'theological assumptions' which underpin anti-women concepts and practices: first, that man is the primary creation and woman is the secondary one, being created from the male rib; second, that woman is responsible for man's fall and expulsion from the Garden of Eden; and third, that woman was created in order to serve the man, therefore she is inferior (Hassan 1995). Hassan's analysis leads her to the conclusion that while these assumptions are made very explicit in the Bible, there is no evidence of them in the Qur'an. In fact, the Qur'anic account of the creation tells us that both man and woman were created for the same purpose: to serve God and humankind. In Hassan's understanding, they stand as equal partners in this duty and are expected to be righteous and protect each other. There is no hierarchy of genders and they are not put in an oppositional relationship (Hassan 1995) because the Qur'an does not differentiate between the creation of man and the creation of woman, which are instead described in 'completely egalitarian terms' (Hassan 2001: 61). Hassan (1988) in her analysis of the Prophetic Traditions referring to creation of humankind, proposes that some Ahadith that go against the spirit and teachings of the Qur'an be rejected, along with those regarded as weak or questionable.

She argues that upon examination, the six Ahadith that mention woman's creation out of man's rib can be proven weak in regard to the chain of transmitters (*isnad*) (Hassan 2001). In her work, Hassan demonstrates how the Ahadith and the Qur'an become diffused with each other in a common knowledge of Islamic tradtions, and suggests that this confusion has led to obscuring the egalitarian message of the Qur'an.

Barlas (2004, 2006) approaches the Qur'an intent on reading and understanding it in a liberating (socially just) way. She observes that in all religions there have been different readings of sacred texts, and because Islam does not sanction clergy, nobody has the right to monopolize the right to interpret the Qur'an. Posing the question, 'how to read the Qur'an for liberation from patriarchy?', Barlas prepares the ground for her developed argument, and proceeds to give examples of such liberatory readings. The first thing she establishes is her understanding of the Qur'an's attitude to patriarchy. She argues that the Qur'an does not advocate patriarchy: first, the principle of God's unity (*Tawhid*) means that God is indivisible, as is God's sovereignty, hence patriarchal theories that assume male rule of women and children misrepresent males as intermediaries between women and God and are therefore theologically unsound; second, God is just to all humankind, therefore God's word cannot teach misogyny or injustice (*Zulm*) to anyone;[6] third, she points out that God is beyond gender (is not male, like male, female, like female, neuter, or like neuter) and therefore there is no special affinity between God and males. Thus, Barlas argues (2006) that the Qur'an rejects the notion of a patriarchalized God. Barlas derives the three methodological principles of reading the Qur'an from the Qur'an itself: textual holism, reading for the best meanings, and using analytical reasoning in interpretation. The Qur'an requires that it is read as a unity, therefore using verses 'out of context' is erroneous (Barlas 2006: 15). The Qur'an itself states that it is polysemic, therefore it needs to be read in order to recover justice 'broadly conceived' (Barlas 2006: 16) and that there is a need to use one's own reason and intellect to reveal the Quran's meanings. Barlas explores intertextuality (internal relationships of texts) and extratextuality (the context of reading) of the Islamic sources and texts used in Islamic discourses. She shows that semiotic polyvalence of many Arabic words make it extremely difficult (or impossible) to deliver a faithful translation of the Qur'an. In addition, she questions the use of extra-Qur'anic sources to explain meanings in it, which, she believes, is an important issue for women since misogynous readings were 'derived mostly from (...) the Tafsir and Ahadith' (Barlas 2006: 37). To sum up,

Barlas advocates that all believers should read and interpret the sources themselves, as the Qur'an itself provides a methodology by which to read and understand it.

Wadud names her strategy of reading the Qur'an in the context of fulfilling *khilafah*, or God's trusteeship on Earth and occurring as a 'spiritualist moral existentialist perspective addressing the question of being' (2000: 21). She understands khilafah as human obligation on earth for the sake of Allah, which, in her view, women need to start fulfilling. She asserts that re-reading the Islamic sources is necessary as neo-traditionalists claim that in Islam, women's rights are not problematic. Wadud argues that there are three different phenomena which are understood as 'Islam', and that they are often conflated. The first, fundamental one is Islam at the level of primary sources: the Qur'an and the *Sunnah*. The second one is Islamic exegesis, law, ethics, philosophy and aesthetics built upon the two primary sources, usually by male scholars. The third is lived Islam, which draws from the first two levels and also from cultural contexts. It comes in 'various permutations and complex configurations' (Wadud 2000: 4). To identify the pristine principles of Islam, free from male voices, women's readings of Islamic sources are required. She argues that through prohibition of the female voice in the process of Islamic exegesis, khilafah has been violated. In Wadud's view, the process of female reinterpretation must begin with the Qur'an due to its unprecedented intellectual and moral significance. The integrity of the Islamic worldview will then be sustained through fair and just action.

Barazangi (2000: 40) links the concept of khilafah to the authority to interpret Islamic scriptures. She writes: 'Knowledge, particularly religious knowledge, means authority, and religious authority means power'. Therefore, she argues, only knowledgeable Muslim women are able to self-identify as *khalifah* (trustees) within Islam. The question of legitimacy is significant, also in terms of online Islamic contexts, in the sense that it urges us to consider who can produce new interpretations of Islamic texts. In classical Islamic scholarship, the person engaging in interpretation had to be educated in traditional Islamic sciences (MacDonald 2005). Mernissi (1992) criticizes this requirement as it limits the group of interpreters to male histographers and theologians, who have monopolized Islam for their own political purposes.

Results of interpretations offered by Hassan (1988), Mernissi (1992) and An-Na'im (2002) may be seen as problematic, as they all propose leaving out certain Ahadith, which to mainstream believers would constitute an unlawful innovation prohibited by the Qur'an. However, the question whether or not mainstream believers are as inflexible in accepting legitimacy of various interpretations (including the reformist ones), as MacDonald suggests, remains unclear. There is a claim that Islamic authority is undergoing atomization due to increased dissemination of different types of Islamic knowledge on the Internet. This allows speculation that individual engagement (reading, interpreting, and applying one's own interpretations of Islamic sources) may be becoming more acceptable (Anderson 1999).

Notably, the debates within and about Islamic feminism and the analyses of subtle differences in the individual understandings of the term have been the hallmark of academia and the educated classes. Badran (1996: 3) writes: 'The history of Egyptian feminism has been about middle and upper class women assuming agency'. These women were traditionally privileged, possessing financial resources, education and the time to engage in discussions of gender politics in their respective societies. El Saadawi (1993) suggests that they have paid no attention to the grievances of poor working women. I argue that technological development, especially the emergence of the 'new media', and better access to education for women, has the potential to change the nature of these debates, as more women (including those with no connections to academia or elites) can participate more widely, with the Internet making debates more inclusive.[7] Technology is increasingly available, even for those with a low socioeconomic status, as Internet cafes are commonplace in developing countries. There are even women-only establishments allowing devout women to surf the Web in a non-intimidating atmosphere (Abu Romi 2008). In addition, the use of the Internet is popularized by educational institutions which offer computer facilities to their students (Skalli 2006). As the Internet is becoming more multilingual, some women's online communications are held in 'ASCII-ized' Arabic – Arabic typed using Roman characters (Palfreyman and Al-Khalili 2003). However, the answer to the question as to whether more women across the class divide have seized the opportunity to engage in specific Islamic gender debates online is, as yet, unknown.

Women in online Islamic environments

Online Islamic environments are thriving; researchers have begun to explore how they have been developed and what implications this has had. The first studies expressed incredulity that technology can be used for such a 'non-scientific' purpose as religion:

> Because of a Western tendency to distinguish between technical and spiritual matters, the use of high-tech communications for religious purposes continues to seem noteworthy to secularists when they initially encounter it, but from Indonesia to Morocco, e-mail and the Internet foster new and rapid forms of communication and coordination for the religiously minded. (Eickelman and Anderson 1999: 4)

However, the amount of theoretically driven empirical research on online expressions of Islam is still scant in comparison with the amount of available data (Ho *et al.* 2008). The debate on the impact of new technologies upon Islamic practices and exegesis is twofold: one position is that the media allows the extension of traditional religious authority; the other argues that media opens new spaces for debate and a subsequent democratization of religious authority (Hirschkind 2001). Although these two processes are often considered mutually exclusive, they are likely to happen concurrently. Here I focus on the latter position suggesting that the religious authority in Islam is becoming atomised and 'reframed' (Anderson 1999), as new interpreters and interpretations are growing in numbers. Anderson takes a historical perspective on this phenomenon and argues that the process was initiated when Muslim students of technical subjects went abroad and became 'diaspora pioneers' in the West.[8] Facing the lack of traditional guidance from Islamic scholars, they resorted to the Internet to create networks of contacts and applied methods acquired earlier in the course of their study to address religious issues. This has led to the development of 'creolized discourses' which denotes discourses created out of two, or more, separate communities of communication. 'Creolization' is a term Anderson (1999: 44) uses for mixed Islamic content, juxtaposed intellectual techniques, and a whole range of Muslim Internet users who are not characterized by the sender/ receiver binary, but instead form a community which is creative and receptive at the same time.

Anderson lists groups that have produced alternative Islamic discourses online, and apart from the students of technical subjects, he mentions 'other' academics (possibly those working in the arts, humanities and social sciences): professionals, student associations, activists and non-mainstream schools of Islam, like Sufis. All of them have contributed to a widened public sphere of debate and discussion, and developed a meeting ground for different discourses. Anderson (2002: 302) writes that such interaction between Islamic discourses is not new; that 'the often detached Islam of the madrasa and more engaged, more socially embedded, vernacular expressions of religiosity' were often bridged by intermediate communities. These intermediate contexts reflect 'a more nuanced diversity of views, settings, projects and expressions of Islam today' (Anderson 1999: 53). In consequence, new social agents may lay claim to Islamic authority (Mandaville 2007).

Whereas many observations Anderson (1999) makes are relevant, he fails to address separately the online presence of a significant group of believers: Muslim women. While they may constitute a part of the groups he mentions, he does not address the ways in which women's discourses may be important but different from all others. One cannot judge from Anderson's writing whether Muslim women have created their own online spaces and discourses that would affect the public sphere on the Internet or where women's Islamic discourses on the continuum between elite and mass Islam are situated.

Bunt, in his first book on online Islamic environments, *Virtually Islamic*, does not cover women's online presence either, but he notes that 'women's issues and Islam online are a significant area for further study' (2000: 71). In his next book, *Islam in the Digital Age*, Bunt (2003: 209) further addresses the importance of research into online discourses on gender issues in Islam:

> The extent to which the Internet is opening up new channels of communication for marginalised groups remains an area requiring further detailed research, especially in association with gender issues. Questions which still need to be approached include how Muslim women are applying the medium in relation to Islam, and whether typologies of female Cyber Islamic Environments are emerging; alternatively, are women being 'relegated' to section within sites, or being simply content rather than content originators? ... The issue of Muslim women on the Internet is a very important one, which the writer hopes will be fully researched by appropriate specialists in the field. For reasons of ethics and gender, the writer did not wish to enter as a researcher or anonymous passive observer into the areas of all-female Muslim cyberspace (for example, mailing lists and chatrooms) that could be defined by some as e-hijab (covered) or e-haram (forbidden)

This author makes three important points: first, he identifies the area as requiring further research. Since the publication of his books in 2000 and 2003, little has been published further on the subject, although the body of research on Muslim women's online presence is steadily growing. The second point he addresses is sensitivity of the subject of Muslim women's online presence, which requires much ethical consideration. Bunt suggests here that, as a man, he did not feel justified to research exclusively female environments, which might be a breach of the Islamic code of behaviour. Finally, he suggests that such environments exist, and are 'researchable' (for someone else, under different conditions).

My research project on Muslim women's newsgroups attempts to address this research gap. In the further sections of this chapter I analyse other work on Muslim women's activities in different contexts: blogs, discussion groups and websites which provide some answers to Bunt's questions. Bunt's two studies flag up Muslim women's presence on the Internet, and he makes a pertinent distinction between their presence as 'content' and as 'content creators' (2003: 209). In his exploration of Islamic expressions online, he provides a good delineation of women-related material. In his discussion of the complexities of online manifestations of political Islam, he reports the existence of responses to gender issues in the Muslim world in the form of websites such as 'The Revolutionary Association of Women of Afghanistan',[9] which highlights the injustices that the Afghani people face. Bunt (2000: 72) notes that there is a statement displayed on the website where the authors state their belief that the injustices are 'due to politics and ignorance, not Islam' and they are clearly against religious fanatics who they call 'bandits'. In this case, women are both the creators and the content, taking an active role in the production of the discourse on the status of the Muslim woman.

Bunt (2003: 209) provides an example of a website where women are, in his words, 'the content' (2003: 209). This is the Internet outlet of the Jama'at-I Islami Pakistan organization which includes writings on women's 'intellectual and spiritual status' as well as on the issues of marriage, divorce and inheritance. While the website's author suggests that he is in favour of gender equality which has been introduced by Islam, his piece accuses the West and western feminism of attempts to produce a 'he-woman', deprived of 'feminine identity and character' (Bunt 2000: 76). This statement suggests a lack of recognition of the different kinds of western feminism observed by Barlas (2004). The authors suggest that the situation of women in Pakistan could be improved by giving women a 'decisive role in the political parties, election and decision-making in the assemblies' (Bunt 2000: 78). They also claim that 'women should be provided adequate environment and facilities to protect their rights and undertake social up-lift plans' (Bunt 2000: 78). Although the quotation suggests that increasing the recognition of women's Islamic rights is one of the organization's objectives, it is listed alongside issues such as motorway provision. Therefore, although from a woman's point of view it is a much improved design for the role of women in Pakistani society, the website still remains a predominantly male interpretation of where women should be active and to what extent.

Bunt (2003) also explores widespread fatwa websites, where scholars answer believers' questions about Islam. The fatwas/fatawa are stored in archives and divided into categories. Often one of the categories is called 'Women's Issues' and contains the following subsections: 'Beautification', 'Clothing', 'Breastfeeding', *'Hijaab'*, *'Mahram'*, 'Menstruation', and 'Worship'. Women's issues are one of the largest areas of interest in another fatwa website that Bunt indicates.

Bunt's studies indicate his interest in online discourses on women's rights in Islam, but the first study of Muslim women's activity online was conducted by Bastani (2001). She explored patterns of online interaction among Muslim women participating in a women-only transnational Anglophone newsgroup (online discussion group) called the Muslim Women's Network (MWN). Bastani states that the women came together because of their shared Islamic faith and the newsgroup was established to 'provide a forum to engage in an intellectual discourse on significant contemporary issues that impact on Islam, especially those pertaining to, or affecting, women' (2001: 42). Bastani's respondents are proud that they are using technology to their advantage and specify some other benefits in addition to learning about Islam: support from other newsgroup members, advice, having someone to talk to, making friends. Bastani's research indicates that such online groups have support and advisory functions which are framed by Islamic beliefs: members explain that efforts spent on helping others are repaid in much greater proportion by Allah. Bastani argues that above all, 'MWN members use the network to express ... their identity as Muslim women' (2001: 58). They do so in a number of ways: they use Arabic/Islamic pseudonyms and phrases; they tell their stories of engagement in Islam and, in the case of converts, stories of their 'journey to Islam'; they exchange prayers; they are able to 'connect' with other Muslim women and discuss shared issues. Bastani gives some examples of discussion subjects: 'gender and equity'; 'hijab and discrimination'; 'hand shaking'; 'mixing of genders'; 'child care'; 'helping others'. Members consult each other, and usually they receive a reply which considers what the Islamic sources say about these issues. Bastani refers to the concept of the *pool of social capital,* indicating that members who are helpful to others are not only likely to receive some help in return, but they also improve their position in the group hierarchy (and thus increase their pool of social capital). Women who are geographically isolated from larger Muslim communities are the most active members of the online group and have high levels of social capital – it is suggested that high activity in online newsgroups like this one can reduce feelings of isolation and anxiety. Bastani, however, does not address the concept of Islamic charitable acts (Kochuyt 2009) which could also be helpful in understanding why women are so willing to help other members of the group.

Bastani's participants are comfortable expressing their Islamic identity as in the group they have a deep sense of belonging. Here they are able to share their concerns about the difficulty of leading a religious life in a predominantly secular western society. For example, they write about how difficult it is to celebrate *Eid ul-Fitr* on a work day, or how annoying it is to be unable to find an Islamic school in the vicinity to send their children to.

In her research, conducted in a very different cultural and political context, Brouwer (2004) arrives at similar conclusions. She analyses Dutch Muslim mixed-gender online communities. First of all, the discussion forum she explores is also related to a geographic location, so members are able to share practical information on Islamic issues, such as local *halal* shops, mosques, times of prayers and Islamic schools. Gender and the position of women in Islam seem to be the subject of heated arguments. In her account of the online discussions, Brouwer relates men's views in greater length: her account suggests that while women ask, men tend to feel they can legitimately give authoritative answers. She reports that men were likely to criticize individual interpretations of Islam and propagate traditional interpretations. However, an example of a woman who successfully challenged a 'male view' on women's position in Islam by trying to broaden the discussion and include her views on men's position in Islam is given.

Brouwer elaborates on women's views in another case study, entitled 'Giving Voice to Dutch Moroccan Girls on the Internet' (Brouwer 2006). This title may be considered rather debatable (because it is not clear who gives the girls the voice as they seem to have employed it themselves). One of the important points she makes is that although much has been written about Muslim women, little draws from direct contact with them – and she suggests that researching Muslim women's online communities allows the opportunity of direct contact. Yet it is not entirely clear whether

Brouwer intends to challenge the imagery of the 'oppressed Muslim woman'. In one paragraph she describes a 'stereotype [of Muslim women] set forth by the Western media' (2006: np), but further down, she sums up some existing research on 'oppressed voices' and argues that 'Muslim girls in the Netherlands are victims of forced marriages, arranged by their families, or victims of beatings by their fathers or husbands' (2006: np).

Her participants seek similar benefits from the participation in online discussions as do Bastani's: they debate about issues such as headscarves and gender-mixing; seek out the company of other people of the same ethnic background, or other Muslims; and express their identity by employing Arabic/Islamic sounding nicknames. The discussions about Islamic issues also involve an examination of Islamic sources in the quest for a right interpretation and sharing concerns about 'negative western attitudes'. Brouwer writes that Dutch-Muslim girls contest the male dominance in Muslim communities; unfortunately she does not provide any quotes from these conversations. She reports, however, that girls in the discussion group experience verbal abuse from boys intent on disrupting their discussions because they believed that the girls' place was 'in the kitchen'. The importance of the forum in this case was that it gave the girls a chance to argue back using Islamic sources. Brouwer's description of the forum contains a reference to the 'third space' (2005: 72) , a term associated with the work of Homi Bhabha (1994), here understood as a space where Muslim women can discuss all religious issues without interference of the West or other Muslims who might want to deny them that freedom. Muslim women are referred to as 'active agents' in the online world, while being marginalized by the West and 'their own communities' offline.

While Bastani and Brouwer provide accounts of Muslim women's online contestation of discriminating, patronizing discourses, whether western or Muslim ones, they do not provide actual quotes containing their contestation strategies, which would make their work more comprehensive. However, this strategy was employed by Bhimji (2005), who includes data illustrating online interactions between Muslim women and men. Her analysis addresses discussions on language and gender where women and men do not constitute two separate or antagonistic categories. It focuses on discursive forms used by female users of online Islamic spaces to subvert the stereotype of passive and silent Muslim women. Furthermore, she notes the importance of linguistic practices in the transformation from Muslim to 'Islamite' (the process of constructing a new religious self in modern contexts), because the use of language is an important marker of identity formation. By setting up such a context for her research, she links newly established religious identities to the online discussions on Islam. One of her most interesting findings is that female participants in the online discussions on Islamic sites are no less vocal than the males (Bhimji 2005); in contrast, there is a considerable body of research that argues that typical female users of the Internet have very different patterns of communications to those of male users, and contribute less to mixed-gender discussions (Jackson *et al.* 2001), and are often silenced, sexually harassed, and flamed[10] (Barak 2005). The power structure in Islamic online environments appears to be much more egalitarian, and women behave assertively, defending their hermeneutic positions in an articulate way.

One of Bhimji's participants states that she has the right to dislike popular music and prefers to listen to recitations of the Qur'an; later, she challenges a male discussant who calls her preferences uneducated and backward: 'Brother with all due respect I have a right to my own opinions on this' (Bhimji 2005: 211). Another woman responds to a man who used the phrase 'what the hell': 'I found that kind of rude ... but I guess that is just how you are' (Bhimji 2005: 210). It is not clear whether Bhimji's choice of the former quote was dictated by the fact that it contained a very clear woman's objection to a post of a man who then tried to convince her she was wrong; or by the fact that a woman stated that she preferred a very strict interpretation of Islam which rejected popular music, while the man appeared more 'liberal' because he did not have anything against popular music. Yet, in spite of his 'liberal' beliefs, he continued to try to impose his view on the female participant, essentially denying her the right to her own opinion, which indicated that he was not so liberal after all.

This exchange indicates that perhaps even if women do not explicitly express opinions in favour of equality, their non-conformist and authoritative performance in mixed-gender environments is a sign that they enact equality. Bhimji reports that women enter and start debates on Islamic issues, such as the validity of Wahhabi sect scholarship, backing up their argument with Qur'anic references and also referring to previous relevant debates. To emphasize their point, they use irony, ask rhetorical questions or simply explain exactly why their perspective on discussed issues is different from other members. Furthermore, they use emoticons/ smiley faces and large colourful fonts to indicate their emotional state (anger, cheerfulness). In the process of building their Islamic identity they also employ Islamic/Arabic vocabulary, such as *Alhamdulillah* (with God's blessings) or *Jazakallah* (may God reward you).

The significance of Bhimji's research lies in the fact that she gives an account of women participating in an Islamic online forum as agents of knowledge. They engage in debates on a level that Bhimji (2005: 218) pertinently calls 'deeper than the merely cursory'. She reports that women use a very advanced Islamic vocabulary and discuss complex theological concepts. Such well-developed and justified arguments are satisfactory for the entire community, as they often remain unchallenged. Bhimji shows that the linguistic practices of these Muslim women debunk two stereotypes: those of a passive and submissive female Internet user and of a silent, subordinate Muslim woman. Furthermore, by giving numerous examples of women's statements she identifies well-developed techniques women use to justify their views and to contest the views of others. Bhimji's research suggests that Muslim women engage in the interpretation of Islamic sources online on a wider scale; however, she does not assess the scale of this phenomenon.

Muslim women get involved in online debates on both Islamic understandings and political issues. Rahimi (2008: 41, emphasis added), analysing the effect of the Internet technologies on the shape of political expression, writes: 'Probing the freedom provided by the Internet, Internet users – *especially women* – are finding in blogs an alternative medium for expression that is denied to them in physical public spaces'. However, he does not provide the characteristics of the women's expressions, which, given the specificity of the women's situation in Iran, must sometimes reflect different concerns to those of men's. Female Iranian bloggers have gained considerable fame in the West, where they are the topic of radio shows (BBC Radio Four 2008) and newspaper articles (e.g. Hermida 2002). There are also similar pieces on Saudi women's blogging in the popular media (e.g. Abou-Alsamh 2006).

Amir-Ebrahimi (2008a, 2008b) in her analysis of Weblogistan (the Iranian blogging space) writes about women's increasing visibility in society which they achieve through the active use of the online public sphere. She argues that women's self-disclosures, which take place on their blogs, are considered a transgression of *urf* (customs and social conventions) as well as religious edicts (Amir-Ebrahimi 2008b). This leads to online attacks and repression by those who do not tolerate women's visibility, even in online public spaces (*Daily Telegraph* 2008). This is the reason why women often write under pseudonyms, fearing for their personal security. However, women who write in more mainstream socio-political blogs do so under their own names in order to be more transparent and politically effective (Amir-Ebrahimi 2008b).

There are interrelated areas in which the use of the Internet is useful for Muslim women activists, for example, it permits access to uncensored information (although the Internet does not remain free from interventions such as government crackdowns, site close-downs and user repression; Alavi 2005), so that information retrieval is more cost and time effective; it increases the number of women's voices, initiatives, and activities on all levels without them having to rely on traditional media; finally, it encourages women to network, forge alliances and broaden the scope of their interventions (Skalli 2006). Amir-Ebrahimi sees the advantage of women's blogging in that it makes the female narrative seem *more ordinary*. In the example she evokes to demonstrate this, some Iranian women recently blogged about their reflection on their sexual experiences, which was received with encouragement from many fellow bloggers; this reaction was a completely new phenomenon in the Iranian blogosphere These blogs are also a window into genuine expressions of femininity for men who, living in sexually-segregated societies, may not have a chance to learn about the diversity of female perspectives on many issues. Amir-Ebrahimi (2008b) writes about Iranian men commenting on female blogs, where they confess their ignorance in sexual relations and lack of knowledge about their own masculinity – this is another small revolution in gender relations as formerly unmentionable issues can be addressed on a more open and equal basis.

Whereas numerous female bloggers challenge the image of a 'decent girl', contrary to general opinion, many others are young, veiled and religious (Amir-Ebrahimi 2008b). They are also looking for opportunities to express themselves in ways that propagate their religious beliefs and positions (Amir-Ebrahimi 2008a). Although in the traditional understanding, blogging is in contradiction to the definition of a religious woman, who should avoid putting herself in the public view, some female religious bloggers take their public presence even further, putting up photographs of themselves next to their blog entries. This is particularly true of entries which discuss the significance of hijab. One of them, the author of 'The Journal of the Wife of a Cleric' commented on the famous women's school in Qom, the Jame'at-ol Zahra, and became a celebrity in the Iranian blogosphere. Another author, this time a daughter of a cleric, wrote about her frustration related to always being defined by her father and ironically entitled her blog 'The Journal of a Daughter of a Cleric'. These girls are daughters of the women who were fighting in the Islamic Revolution of 1979, and and so often grew up with a female role model who acted as a pious woman of authority in the household, a woman defined by her own activities. The daughters have also developed a sense of individuality and agency, which can be seen in the blogs. Fatemeh, one of the blogging girls described by Amir-Ebrahimi (2008a) wants to become a religious scholar; therefore she is studying for the entrance exams to the Qom school, while the entire family share the housework. Another girl describes herself as an 'antitraditional and unconventional antifeminist' and reflects on wearing a face veil. Her struggle, she writes, is to challenge those people who think that face veil wearers are submissive and traditional women without agency – therefore she presents herself as an autonomous individual who is at the same time against the western concept of feminism.

Iranian women's blogs enable them to contest patriarchal traditions or express their Islamic beliefs on a wide scale without having to rely on the traditional media. In addition, these blogs constitute an entirely new opportunity to look into Iranian women's personal thoughts, ideas and feelings. The blogosphere, therefore, constitutes a valuable resource for the study of 'ordinary' women's perceptions of social and political contexts in Iran. Furthermore, the Iranian example demonstrates the opportunity for political engagement by Muslim women afforded by the Internet in authoritarian states.

Websites and blogs are extensively used by Muslim women across the world to express their views, explode myths and stereotypes, and oppose dominant discourses which are aimed at controlling them. These sites enable consolidation and mobilization of women who use their subversive power and produce oppositional public discourses. A website created by the Revolutionary Association of Women of Afghanistan (RAWA) is a space where a group of Afghan Muslim women protest against women's oppression. They meticulously present cases of women who are abused, brutalized, deprived of healthcare, impoverished and so desperate that they commit self-immolation. The RAWA website allows interaction in the guestbook, and this is where two dominant discourses compete to undermine the narratives produced by the RAWA women. The first one is a specific form of neo-Orientalism, a confrontational ideology that draws from anti-Islamic sentiment and presents Islam as inherently conflicted with modernity and democracy (Niva 1998). Guestbook entries representing a neo-Orientalist approach suggest that, for example, Afghan women should 'get off their buts (sic) and do something', 'stop wearing the burqua (sic)' and 'stop blaming the US' (Bickel 2003: np). These neo-Orientalist proponents see the US army in Afghanistan, using Spivak's (1987: 297) phrase, as 'white men saving brown women from brown men'.

The second discourse, produced by quasi-religious extremists, accuses the RAWA women of betraying Islam in favour of the West and has strong misogynist undertones. Individuals posting to the guestbook in this spirit threaten to bring women 'under control' through 'purification' and 'female circumsison' (sic) (Bickel 2003: np). These entries contain very strong, offensive language which indicates aggression and brutal power. Both these discourses expect Afghan women to side with them in the perceived combat between Western and Islamic values as well as in the real military conflict between the allied forces and the Taliban. However, the RAWA women create discourses which simultaneously challenge the former two. They refuse to take sides in the conflict; instead, they state that the US presence in Afghanistan is unlawful occupation, that in no way can result in establishing a democratic state; that the Taliban, allegedly in the name of Islam, have brought oppression, torment, and poverty; finally, they accuse national and international NGOs of corruption. Through these statements they criticize the attempts of all these agents to control and interfere with women's lives. The women of RAWA advocate an alternative third way, which would entail establishing a secular democratic state with the aid of the freedom- and independence-loving people of Afghanistan. However, they embrace Islam as their religion, albeit one which they see as appropriated and abused by quasi-religious extremists who use it as an excuse to control women. Their slogan is 'Neither the US nor Jehadies and Taliban, Long Live the Struggle of Independent and Democratic forces of Afghanistan!' The Internet enables Afghan women to engage on a political level, maintain a defined, powerful political identity and publicize their viewpoint at the current sociopolitical level.

The area of Muslim women's activity on the Internet is still largely unexplored, although there are many indicators that it is growing and becoming increasingly differentiated. All studies of Muslim women's online discussions carried out to date emphasize the following points: that Muslim women find the Internet a useful tool for a range of purposes, be it arguing in debates on Islam, discussing ways they are misunderstood and misrepresented in the West, or partaking in political struggles. It is perhaps an obvious statement that every woman may have different reasons for using the Internet, but the diversity of activities that Muslim women engage in online demonstrates the range and extent of issues they have to or choose to face and deal with; as Amir-Ebrahimi writes: 'Through bold narration in their blogs, they [Iranian female bloggers] revealed first-hand information about themselves which had never before been told publicly' (2008b: 93).

Muslim women's challenges of both the neo-Orientalist discourse and the patriarchal discourse claiming to be Islamic can be observed in most studies on Muslim women's online expressions. The fact that they construct a third, oppositional *public* discourse suggests that the Internet may turn out to be more helpful in creating new discourses than the scepticists, such as Roy (2004), have envisaged. Without being overenthusiastic, and bearing in mind many of the reservations that Muslim women may have in relation to the Internet, such as widespread pornography, violence, and Islamophobic prejudice, the discussed literature demonstrates that the Internet has opened up new opportunities for Muslim women and they have used them to their best interest. The paucity of research into Muslim women's online activities pointed out by Bunt (2003) and Ho *et al.* (2008) suggests that there is still a gap to bridge, especially in regard to new 'online' readings of Islamic texts that may be the next step in researching Muslim women's voices. While the gap in literature on Muslim women's online voices in local contexts (The Netherlands, United Kingdom, Iran, Afghanistan) is closing, there is little research on Muslim women's global expressions and connections produced on international forums and across boundaries; this book is an attempt to investigate this previously unexplored transnational context.

Notes

1 Balchin (2003) argues that most Muslim communities understand feminism as secular and mostly hostile to religion, therefore they do not wish to engage with it. Given that 'Muslim' is an adjective that means in Arabic 'one that submits to God' (Esposito 2002: 153), it is surprising that Barlas equates 'Muslim feminism' with a secular women's movement.

2 Weak (*da'if*) refers to traditions whose chain of narrators was only limited to one authority (Mejia 2007).

3 Islamism is a term often incorrectly confused with Islam, however, boundaries between the two are sometimes blurred. Its many definitions emphasize its grounding in politics. Broadly, Islamism may be understood as a movement of Muslims who draw upon the belief, symbols and language of Islam to inspire, shape, and animate political activity (Pelletreau 1996). Such political activity may be based on moderate, traditional or reactionary thought, reflecting all political fractions and views of Muslims. MacDonald rejects the term 'Islamism' altogether and uses instead "religio-political groups" on the grounds that it is more transparent (2007: 34). Karam's (1998) use of the term 'Islamist feminists' emphasizes the belief that gender equality is a West-originating term which should be replaced with gender complementarity and justice, as some rights and responsibilities of Muslim men and women are different (but equally important). Thus, she suggests

that Islamist feminists get involved in gender politics by rejecting western concepts and values.

4   However, across the Muslim world, the notion that women should be confined to the home sphere is less strong than critics of Islam would like to suggest (Falah 2005). This notion is stronger in rural, uneducated societies (Ahmad and Aijaz 1993) where the resistance to women's emancipation is likely to be cultural. In urban areas, women, regardless of their position on gender equality, tend to have opportunities to be active in political organizations and gain considerable influence within them (Abdelatif and Ottaway 2007).

5   For examples of disputed Ahadith see Barlas (2006) and Farooq (2007).

6   Barlas (2006: 14) argues that the concept of women's inferiority breeds misogyny, and by the justification of women's subordination, patriarchies "violate women's [Islamic] rights by denying them agency and dignity, principles that the Qur'an says are intrinsic to human nature itself".

7   However, there are still those without access to technology and schooling, and these are excluded from such debates due to lack of resources and/or education.

8   Until recently the vast majority of Islamic online discourses were produced in the diaspora as penetration levels were low in Muslim-majority countries (Mandaville 2007).

9   www.rawa.org (accessed on 21 May 2009).

10   There is some research that states that gender affects online interaction in a more complex way. For example, Li (2006) finds that women tend to use challenging language more than men. Similarly, Witmer and Katzman (1997) find that women in their sample challenge and flame men more often.

2 Participants' methodologies of engaging with Islamic sources

In Chapter 1 I explored existing categorizations of Muslim women's epistemological positions on Islamic knowledge, defined by their beliefs, values, methodological approaches and justifications rooted in Islamic sources (Hacinebioglu 2007). These studies indicate that there are a variety of stands taken by women, with supporters active in their own environments but rarely communicating with advocates of different understandings, considering them either too lenient or too extreme (Karam 1998; Abdelatif and Ottaway 2007; Ramadan in Karim 2008). In this chapter I identify women's hermeneutic positions on the basis of different approaches to Islamic education and interpretation of sources. Thus, it is a chapter about different methodologies of reading the holy texts employed by the participants. Islamic education is at the heart of believers' engagements with the Qur'an and Ahadith; it also affects the ability of individuals to locate Islamic principles within individual behavioural codes (Shaheed 1986). From the women's point of view, an awareness of their Islamic status is a prerequisite to claiming their God-given rights and defining their identity within the *ummah* and the globalised world.

In the section on Islamic education, I look at the ways women come to individual and shared understandings of Islamic concepts by engaging with Islamic sources and other texts, such as scholars' writings, articles and *fatwas*. I explore different groups' preferences for Islamic sources used to justify opinions and provide solutions to problems and consider the varied modes of engagement with the sources. Finally, I investigate whether women advocating different views on Islamic teachings interact with each other, and if so, in what ways. Through this, I explore the concept of Muslim sisterhood and identity within an online context.

Islamic education

Obtaining knowledge of Islamic sources, interpretations, history and law (Douglass and Shaikh 2004) is one of the most emphasized purposes for Muslim women's online discussions. Halstead (2004: 519) writes: 'at the heart of the Muslim concept of education is the aim of producing good Muslims with an understanding of Islamic rules of behaviour and a strong knowledge and commitment to the faith'. Approaches to education in the newsgroups confirm this; Islamic knowledge is given the absolute priority, compared to other, 'secular' knowledges also provided by Muslim schools; while these are considered important, without a religious basis they do not guarantee righteoussness. Afrah, a newsgroup member writes:

> Anyone can be a graduate, a Phd holder, a super-woman, but when it comes to their religion, what is it that they possess compared to the sahabiyaat[1] (this is what they usually compare themselves to right – how they were)? I know many women, some of my friends even, they are extremely successful, but extremely ignorant in their religion.

Women emphasize that the *deen* (the Islamic way of life) is a prerequisite for all their decisions. The main reason for setting up all the discussed newsgroups, according to their public homepages, is increasing Islamic knowledge. One homepage reads: 'We will learn, grow and share our knowledge of Islam with one another'. Participants frequently hold *halaqas* (lessons) on a range of topics, for which members prepare by reading appropriate materials and later discuss arising issues. A reason given for studying Islam online is that knowledge of Islamic teachings prevents one from making choices that could be un-Islamic, for example, in terms of one's future profession. However, women are aware that not all kinds of Islamic knowledge have the same authority; in response to a member seeking advice on preferable university courses, Zainab writes:

> It's our first most duty to get the CORRECT religious knowledge. We come across many confusing things in our life and if you don't have knowledge, anyone can get you astray. So to anyone whos seeking knowledge, first Deen and then other things. When one completes religious education then he/she can go for something else they are

interested in, but always first religion so that any thing that you are doing wrong (unknowingly) like Bid'ah/shirk etc, which mostly people do unknowingly (despite of calling themselves Muslims), can be eliminated.

In her response, Zainab emphasizes the word 'correct', which indicates that she is warning other women about the existence of other, competing and illegitimate religious knowledges and discourses. She mentions that one should avoid teachings that promote *bid'ah*, innovation, which is combatted particularly fiercely by the Salafi[2] movement (Katz 2008). However, this statement can also be understood as an appeal for careful examination of what is described as 'Islamic', because erroneous knowledge must not be incorporated into one's system of values.

All women in the newsgroups, regardless of their views, expect high scholarly standards in the debates. Their first and foremost requirement is to include Islamic references in the postings that express opinions about proper Islamic conduct or respond to earlier contributions. Postings without such backing are considered as personal opinions and given less attention. One of the converts, Izzah, professing a lack of knowledge, asks about the right of women to drive, and requests advice based clearly on the Islamic commandments. Through this question she demonstrates that she is aware of the weight carried by a reference to Islamic sources:

Can someone help me understand and give me some information from a Surah, etc. as to why it is haram for women to drive? I'm not trying to be disprespectfull (sic) to ask this question, but I am a convert and am still learning about Islam and what I should be doing/ not doing. I like the articles that get posted with specific references on subjects and just wondered, mashallah, if anyone could do the same for this subject.

Izzah constructs her posting in such a way that it is clear that she is not attempting to challenge anyone in the group. By stressing her novice status she indicates that her priority is acquiring correct, source-informed Islamic knowledge. Other participants recognize this request and provide references with interpretations. Participants' understandings in regard to permissibility of women driving are very diverse, and they respond according to their knowledge, worldview and experience. Some challenge the driving ban issued by traditional scholars, others argue that it is permissible to drive in certain situations, or posit that the phenomenon of women driving is in conflict with Islamic principles (this is discussed further in Chapter 4). Just as newsgroup 'veterans' assist converts in studying their new faith, children's Islamic education is promoted by participants regardless of their position. As most participants live in non-Muslim majority countries,[3] their options are often limited. While families living in cosmopolitan cities such as London or New York have a wide choice of Muslim schools (Parker-Jenkins 2002), residents of smaller localities are often restricted to Islamic home-schooling, which is supported by websites such as www.islamichomeeducation. co.uk, and often set up by Muslim mothers seeking alternatives to their children's mainstream education. Newsgroup members argue that they, as mothers, are responsible – both directly and indirectly – for their children's acquisition of Islamic knowledge. Samiyah writes:

> The young are our future and we are responsible for their education (ISLAMIC AND SECULAR) what are we really teaching them. We must remember/realize children hear and see a lot more then we really realize and our lives, household and upbringing have a lot of baring on their lives and what type of MUSLIM CHILD/ADULT they will be.

Samiyah's observation that children 'hear and see a lot more' indicates that she is aware of the potential exposure of Muslim children to un-Islamic values and behaviours. She suggests that a proper upbringing can shield them from that by giving them an ability to make Islam-informed choices. The passing-down of Islamic values ensures their continuity; as a result, Samiyah argues, the integrity of the future ummah is in the hands of mothers, and this is why Islam has bestowed so much respect upon them (Barlas 2006).

Engagement with Islamic sources

Islamic education is widely seen by women as mandatory, in line with the hadith narrated by Muslim: 'Whosoever follows a path to seek knowledge therein, Allah will make easy for him a path to Paradise'.[4] However, there are different understandings of what constitutes 'proper' Islamic education, based on varied understandings of Islamic authority. There is a group of women who argue that every Muslim must individually engage with the Islamic scriptural sources, as the

Qur'an never nominated a single religious authority or insitution which would mediate between believers and God. One of them, Alia, states: 'It is mandatory for Muslim women to study and learn the Deen for themselves, not waiting around for men to tell them. Knowledge of the religion is not a masculine thing – it's a Muslim thing <smile>'.

Women advocating individual engagement with the Islamic sources invoke the example of Aisha, the wife of the Prophet, who had a reputation as one of the best educated Muslims of her time, and who was consulted on religious matters. Her knowledge became an 'important source of information about the early Muslim community, since many of the hadith about Muhammad's attitude towards his wives and the women of the Muslim community are from her hand' (Visser 2002: 188). Many participants argue that Muslim women should follow the example of Aisha[5] and other educated Muslim women, and obtain Islamic knowledge so that their Islamic rights and responsibilities will be known to them:

> *Suhayma*: Aisha, radiallahu 'anha, was not only knowledgeable about the Prophet, peace be upon him, but was a judge. The Sahabah, may Allah be please with them, used to come to her and ask her many questions years after the passing of the Prophet. There have been many other outstanding women in Islam with great knowledge who in turn, educated other women. Not long ago there was an article on this list about the elderly Egyptian woman who was not only haafitha of Qur'an,[6] but taught others as well and had been doing it since she was a young woman.

Aamaal seconds her by writing: 'I agree with you, according to the Quran, men & women have equality & also women are encouraged to seek for a better education'. She sees equality and education as two parallel concepts which remain in a causal relationship. Her declaration indicates that women should have access to education because of the concept of gender equality introduced by the Qur'an, but also because education in Islam safeguards this equality. Islamic education is central for these women because it is integral to effective challenging of patriarchal or misogynist interpretations of Islamic sources which emerged and gained influence after the death of the Prophet. Knowledge of Arabic is considered as key to uncovering the multiple meanings of words from the original version of the Qur'an (translated versions are seen as interpretations of the meanings). Therefore, a large number of women in the newsgroups study Arabic to attain a better understanding of the Qur'an. The translation of verse 4:34, which allegedly allows wife beating, is widely debated from a linguistic point of view:

> *Taroob*: Words in Arabic are based primarily on three letter root words and derivations are changed somewhat by adding letters to them. Examples are sajada (derived from three letter 'sjd'), meaning to prostrate, and masjid, meaning the place where the prostration is done. Similarly daraba ('drb') means to beat and the word in the Qur'an which people have translated as 'beat' is actually adriba ('adrb'). According to the dictionaries where I have been able to find the word adriba the meaning is to abandon, forsake, leave alone – not beat.

Participants are aware that such detailed knowledge of Arabic is a valuable tool for deconstructing interpretations of the Scripture that they do not agree with. Therefore, they go to great lengths to develop their Arabic fluency, even if they do not have access to Arabic classes or native Arabic speakers. The Internet helps, as participants are able to exchange URLs (website addresses) of online Arabic courses and support each other by use of simple Arabic phrases with explanations of their meanings. Ameena requests more Qur'anic verses in Arabic to be circulated within group discussions:

> I was thinking of verses from Qu'ran written in Arabic or Islamic terms would be great ... some people have been adding verses to the bottom of their e-mails in English, would love to see more of these in Arabic too! (or with transliteration if you're not able to type in Arabic)

Wafeeqa supplements Ameena's narrative by saying that it is essential to speak Arabic to understand the Arab culture whose importance lies in the fact that Prophet Muhammad was an Arab; in addition, a number of newsgroup members are married to Arab men and either live in Arab countries or go there to visit. She writes: 'The understanding of these things is expressed in the language. The true understanding of culture is expressed in the language. The language is the heart of the people. If we have not learned the language, we need to find a teacher'. Similarly, Bakarat (1993: 135) argues that 'society is key to understanding religion', simultaneously emphasizing the strong links between Arab identity and

Arabic language. Participants' recognition of these links demonstrates their aspiration to deepen their understanding of the Islamic sources, especially the linguistic nuances. They believe that knowledge of Arabic can improve their ability to interpret the sources and spiritually bring them closer to God.

The second group of women advise against individual engagement with Islamic texts as a means of studying the sources and recommend engagement with interpretations of established Islamic scholars. They warn that individual reading may lead to an erroneous understanding of Islam. They also argue that if an interpretation is incorrect, its author, not the person who applies it to their lives, is responsible for potential un-Islamic behaviour because he was in a better position to recognize what was correct and what was wrong. Khadeeja writes:

> *stick to lectures of scholars and their students*, like one of our noble sister – admin of one sister group said, *'Insha Allah [we] will strive to only share information from those whom we have been instructed to take our religion from*[7] and she won't approve msg other than that source either. i was so happy to see it. may allah make us firm like her. ameen.

Such reliance on scholars advocated by this group of participants is strongly criticised by the first group. Alia wrote in response to Khadeeja: 'It only adds "insult" to "injury" when we hear some women parroting what they have been taught by men about what the roles and rights of women are, instead of quoting what is actually correct'. However, representatives of the second group refuse to unconditionally agree with just any male scholars, whether in favour or against gender equality; women who represent this position do not hesitate to criticise scholars whose teachings they do not agree with. One of them disagrees with an influential male Muslim author and scholar, Jamal Badawi, who has written on gender relations in Islam (see Badawi 1995):

> *Lamya*: Flowery and apologetic explainations such as what Brother Jamal has stated in paragraph 6 (I believe it was numbered 6) about the husband not having superiority over his wife is how we get into this kind of trouble in the first place.

Lamya's comments on Badawi's book are critical; she sees his argument in favour of gender equity[8] as apologetic, in that it appears more acceptable by progressive, presumably 'westernized' Muslims. The trouble she refers to is the Women's Liberation movement, and a perceived breakdown of family values. Thus, Lamya does not hesitate to critique a male scholar, acting contrary to the stereotype of the traditional Muslim woman. The fact that she disapproves of the concept of gender equity (arguing in favour of hierarchical gender relations in Islam, thus standing in opposition to 'progressive Muslims') does not allow labelling her with the tag of voicelessness; on the contrary, she is vocal in her support for her views.

The third group of women emphasize the importance of Islamic education and individual engagement with the sources of Islam, but they accept interpretations from a range of Islamic scholars, some of whom they consider legitimate authorities in regard to Islamic knowledge. They are careful in the selection of scholars they decide to follow, and do not tend to take scholars' reasoning at face value. Such a selective approach ensures that other interpreters' potential erroneous understanding does not negatively impact on the reader's Islamic conduct. Aneesa, writing to her opponent in a discussion on following scholars, expresses a view that deep Islamic knowledge is attainable to lay people and scholars alike:

> Please don't conclude that I mean to say scholars are not correct. True scholars are correct. But my point here is that people who are not scholars, or *not* passed out from great colleges *also may be correct*. In fact, Allah swt made Qur'an for us *all*.

Similarly, women in this group also carefully read the Ahadith, always referring to the Qur'an in case of potential contradictions. They believe that while the Sunnah of the Prophet is very important, the Qur'an remains God's word, central to Islam, which is complete and perfect:

> *Yasmeen*: Please understand that not believing in sunnah of muhammed sal allhu aleihi wasallam is wrong, but it does not mean that you follow everything from authentic ahadeeth man-made books and give final priority to it. It is really enough takes us a lot many years, for us to implement whole of Qur'an. We can only afford to keep hadeeth as reference, and that's because, *Qur'an has got everything. Its perfected for mankind*, it has nothing untouched.

Yasmeen believes that Ahadith, even if authentic, has a lower place in the hierarchy of Islamic texts because it is man-made (the chain of transmission relies on human memory). In a heated discussion another participant, Zahira, explains her methodology of reading the Qur'an and Ahadith. She states that the Qur'an tells Muslims what to do, whereas the Ahadith specifies how to do it, and as an example she gives *salat* (the daily prayer). However, she writes that blind adherence to a hadith is wrong; one should always validate the hadith by referring to the Qur'an, which takes precedence over all man-made sources. The women agree that there are weak Ahadith in certain collections (for example, in Bukhari), but one must not reject the entirety of the Ahadith for that reason. Zahira responds to a question posed in relation to perceived contradictions present in this collection:

And besides, what's so wrong in declaring it to be Saheeh,[9] when it's only an interpretation of the Qur'aan itself. It's not an entirely separate book; it's very much related to the Qur'aan, in that it explains the Qur'aan. It does not go against the Qur'aan in any way. The doubts that you have about contradictions present in Saheeh Bukhaaree, please clear them up with a REAL scholar.

The last sentence in this quote suggests that Zahira believes that prestigous scholars are best equipped to solve problems such as contradictions within Ahadith collections or differences between the Qur'an and Ahadith. However, she does not advise against individual engagement with Islamic sources. In fact, her statement demonstrates that she herself has reflected on the above issues. The fact that both participants consider not only the hierarchy of the Islamic texts but also a methodology of reading them, indicates their deep level of intellectual engagement with the sources. In this discussion the women did not agree on the extent of authority that the Ahadith had. While one of them claimed that because it was human-made, it had 'human' authority, the other cited a verse from the Qur'an, which, in her view, gave the Ahadith divine authority: 'O you who believe! Obey Allaah and obey the Messenger' (4:59). However, they both agree that sects which reject the Ahadith altogether, such as the Mu'tazilis (Al-Qaradawi 2007), are in error, which indicates at least partial consensus between them.

Women in the third group are especially critical of other Muslims' religious ignorance, which they see as the cause of problems in the Muslim community:

> *Afra*: We were born to worship, and how can we worship if we are ignorant of the deen? Many MUSLIMS TODAY ARE EXTREMELY IGNORANT … due to the fact , Lack of Knowledge in and of their deen (…) The more one learns, the more humble they become.

This statement indicates a strong belief in inseparability of faith and Islamic education, which, in turn, makes one more humble in terms of judgement. Humility is an important concept for this group of women, as they do not attempt to force their interpretations on anyone else, and rely on their own understandings of Islamic sources (which may include appropriated interpretations by scholars they agree with). The need to remain humble in faith is also expressed by their acceptance of a number of varied interpretations of the sources.

Quotes in this section indicate that there are both commonalities and differences between participants with regard to various aspects of Islamic education and reading of the sources. They discuss methodologies of reading and hierarchies of the Islamic texts; the question of independent engagement and using existing interpretations, finally, the implications of obtaining both correct and incorrect knowledge or not obtaining it at all. The right to education, also expressed as a responsibility, is unquestioned, in a similar vein to the views of Franks's (2001) respondents.

There are three different positions that emerge from the women's discussions; one group argues for personal, individual engagement with Islamic sources, on the grounds that all Muslims are required to study their religion; another group advocates reliance on scholars' rulings and interpretations, as they regard scholars to be the best equipped in the process of interpretation, having studied not only the Qur'an, but also classical Arabic, Islamic history and law; the third group oscillates between the former two, encouraging others to use critical thinking in reading human-produced Islamic texts, bearing in mind that the Qur'an is central to all other texts.

Islamic texts versus Muslim practices

The 'Islam versus 'culture' debate in Muslim communities, and particularly prominent in non-Muslim majority contexts (Maqsood nd), finds an outlet in women's online discussions. A distinction is made by some Muslims between 'pure Islam' and 'cultural Islam'. 'Culture' in these reflections is understood as a set of pre-Islamic or non-Islamic customs which have been illegitimately incorporated into interpretations of Islam. This, it is argued, has resulted in the emergence of a code of behaviour *branded as Islam* that in reality is a deviation from Islam. Amir-Ebrahimi refers to the similar concept of 'society customs', *urf*, as recognized by the Shari'a (2008b).

The participants argued that Islam was introduced because Arab people needed moral, social and political guidance. The pre-Islamic period is commonly referred to as the 'time of ignorance' or *jahiliyya* (Hawker 2002: 5) which ended with the Revelation of the Qur'an to Muhammad. In the western context, some Muslims claim that it becomes even more important to separate oneself from the local un-Islamic influences and values so as to protect one's purity (Ramadan 1999). Murad states that this position is especially tempting to second- and third-generation Muslims, who find themselves in a cultural vacuum – they feel equally alien to their parents' cultural heritage as to western secularism and consumerism; therefore, they decide to reject the notion of 'culture' altogether (Karim 2008). However, it remains problematic to what extent a decontextualization of religion results in a purification of its practices (Barlas 2006). Some scholars argue that such a take on Islam is simplistic; that Islam becomes universal not through rejection of culture, but through embracing it, which is where, to some extent, its strength lies (Ramadan 1999). Furthermore, it is claimed that Islam was revealed to people of the Arab culture for an important reason, so it should be read through this cultural and historic lens which aids in the understanding of specific injunctions (see e.g. Barlas (2006) for a discussion of hijab from a historical-cultural perspective). Feminist Muslim scholars argue that what needs to be rejected is the exclusivity of male Islamic scholarship which has introduced patriarchal, 'cultural' elements into the complex system of moral, social and legal structures within Islam (Mernissi 1992).

Dovetailing with these academic debates, participants converse about the degree to which the ummah has followed the original teachings of Islam. They address the issues of the 'purity' of Islam, cultural accretions, and differences in Muslim practices across the world. The question of patriarchy emerges in the discussions too, as there are different views among women regarding the realities of gender relations in Islam. In a discussion on the situation of women in Afghanistan, two women represented opposite views on the Taliban rule and argued about its influence on the situation of women:

Maha: The NOTHERN ALLIANCE WAS terrible ... a women could not leave her house without fear that she her breasts would get cut off: (and now ... they want to destroy taliban ... destroy the country who has shariah law ... PROPER shariah law [emphasis hers]. The taliban may not be perfect ... but they are the closest thing to a pure islamic state.

Jeehan: The taliban is close to real islamic shariah?
ru kidding me? hahahaha that absurb ... if they are close to real shariah then i have bluehair! nah sometimes i think theve never even read the quran wit the kr@p they get away with in the name of 'islam'.

Maha: yes, the Taleban upholds Shairah law in most cases. They are the closest thing to a true Islamic state. Don't buy into all the western media please.

Jeehan: well talaban closest to Islamic ... so then to you Islam is about beating women and not allowing them an education? I have met women from there so my info is not from the western media, where is yours from that it is OK for them to treat women that way? It is unislamic of them, women are equal in Islam. Mind you though i do not believe in what the U.S. goverment is doing either and i vote so therefor (sic) i can say what i want to about it.

Such a radical difference in opinions as to what constitutes a 'true Islamic state' is likely to be rooted in varying interpretation of 'pure Islam'. To Maha, the introduction of Shari'a law is a marker of an Islamic state. Although at first she refers to the legal system of Afghanistan as 'PROPER', further emphasized by the use of capital letters, she acknowledges that the Taliban rule is sometimes problematic (the Taliban may be 'not perfect', they uphold Shari'a law in 'most cases'), but sees its potential errors as lesser evils than those promulgated by the West and the Northern Alliance forces, whom she accuses of crimes against women, including severing their breasts. To her, the western coverage of the war in Afghanistan was misrepresentative of the Taliban, showing them as aggressive and misogynistic. Jeehan counters Maha's opinion by claiming that the Taliban do not follow Shari'a law and their rule is just a pretense of an Islamic state. Her view of Taliban rule is that it absolutely goes against the vision of an Islamic state as envisaged by the Prophet Muhammad. Jeehan points out that women's oppression, such as beatings and prohibited access to education, was never his intention, and that he brought women equality, not harm. She denies having her opinions embedded in Western media coverage and argues that she has obtained her information from 'women from there', which gives her a degree of authority in the conversation. The rhetorical techniques she uses to emphasize her point are varied: first, she repeats her opponent's statement in the form of a question, indicating astonishment; then she uses a rhetorical question and includes onomatopoeic laughter, trying to ridicule the other woman's opinion. She further indicates that she does not support that point of view by using strong language, which is disguised by her writing it in a phonetic mode and using keyboard symbols (a common trick of Internet users who wish to swear but want to avoid automatic filtering of strong language on discussion forums). Such an emotional response suggests that she was genuinely apprehensive of Maha's statement. However, after the first rather acerbic response Jeehan explained more mildly and in more detail exactly why she found her opponent's posting misguided.

This dialogue indicates that Maha and Jeehan represent different views on Islamic authority in political and social contexts. Maha sees the Taliban as a political force which dared challenge and tie the western military powers; their continuing influence in Afghanistan is interpreted by her as a result of their religious devotion and is a source of pride to Muslims. Anti-western sentiment is strong in her contribution, and she argues that the willingness of the Taliban to fight the occupying forces and maintain the Islamic identity of Afghanistan redeems them from their misconduct, which she does not dwell on. Instead, she ascribes unspeakable violence against women to the Allied forces, which, she suggests, has been ignored/censored by the western media and only reported by non-western ones.[10]

In contrast, Jeehan rejects the claim that the Taliban rule is Islamic simply because it is presented as Islamic. She suggests that it is instead based on a manipulated interpretation of the Qur'an which has been created exclusively to support violent Taliban policies and actions, especially those directed at women. She refuses to support a political force ostensibly arrayed under the banner of Islam, but, in her eyes, violating the very essence of the religion. The fact that she highlights her own political activity (voting) indicates that she believes in utilizing democratic structures to express an opinion, and perhaps, fight for social and political change. Jeehan's contributions suggest that she does not approach social or political constructs uncritically, leaving unquestioning reverence only to Islamic principles and sources.

Participants address the discrepancy between theory (Islamic sources) and practice (social customs, or 'culture') at both the public/political and private/family levels, which in Islam are closely intertwined (Eickelman and Anderson 1999). Many women see patriarchy as entirely un-Islamic, and refer to men who advocate and participate in patriarchal family and political structures as 'misguided'. According to this group, the belief in men's alleged superiority, sometimes expressed by traditionalist women, is a result of men's manipulation:

> *Aasiya*: Men who adamantly choose to believe and accept this insanity [belief in men's superiority] exploit the naturally submissive nature of women to promote man worship – placing a 'Divine Order' tag on it, as if Almighty God sanctions it. In other words, they deliberately lie on Allah, and have the gall to expect Allah's Blessings! (Allah forbid!)

Women in the newsgroups believe that one of the improvements that Islam has introduced to women's status has been a greater acceptance for widows and divorcees, disregarded in the pre-Islamic period (which is considered by participants as a cultural prejudice). They argue that Prophet Muhammad himself set an example for marrying widows (Khadija, Sawda, Hafsah, Umm Salamah, Juwariya bint al-Harith, Safiyya bint Huyayy), and divorcees (Zaynab bint Jahsh and Umm Habibah), some of whom had children from previous marriages, as well as a woman who after her two previous marriages was both a widow and a divorcee (Maymunah bint al-Harith) (Ahmed 1992: 58). However, women argue that many Muslim men do not follow the Prophet's example and prefer to marry virgins. Kalimah writes: 'there arent that many men who will take a woman who has kids or she's not in her child baring (sic) years or the best one yet is having to consider polygyny because you aren't young, virgin, and fertile'. Similarly, Jeehan writes about a woman who feels she is stuck in an unhappy marriage and does not want to leave her abusive husband: 'divorce is frowned upon (…) she is a mother of two young boys. It is very slim pickings out there for a woman in her situation'. However, in another discussion where the issue of remarriage after divorce is raised, a different opinion is offered. Asma, a member from a Muslim-majority country, posts a question to the group regarding the course of action she should take having been abandoned by her husband. She is encouraged to move to the United States in order to marry a convert; the twi women agree that it is culture (in the sense of 'local customs') that are preventing her from finding happiness:

Nida: Have you thought of marrying a muslim from the U.S.? Converts here are masha'Allah very good. He would support your child and give you your rights.

Asma: (…) as for my problem is yes its mostly culture coz born muslims can [be] sometimes mean its inherited and not really belief so they dont really care what Allah would want them to be. And yes this [moving to the US] could [be] one solution but i dont think there will be an american who would marry a divorced egyptian as iam nt as pretty as u all are:)

Nida: If you feel this is an option there are many brothers over here who would be willing to marry you and take care of your son. Masha'Allah the brothers in my community here are very good and caring with children. All the kids love them.

This discussion touches upon remarriage after divorce as a part of the 'Islam vs culture' debate which here overlaps with the debate on converts and 'born Muslims' (addressed in more detail in Chapter 6). First of all, the women oppose Asma's declaration that she has no chances of getting remarried and encourage her to travel to the USA. As her first husband abandoned her and their child, she seems to have lost trust in men, so the other women praise Muslim men they know personally and state that the men participate willingly in the raising of children and doing the housework. One of the women even offers her practical help on arrival. However, Nida's comment about converts suggests that in her view a Muslim convert would be better for Asma as he would have learnt the Islamic teachings in a context free from the patriarchal traditions that permeate Asma's community. Therefore, she implies that a convert would not be against marrying a divorcee with a child, as this would be *sunnah* (in accordance with the life of the Prophet, hence highly advisable). Asma voices her critical view on 'born Muslims', suggesting that their religion is inherited, and as Islam may not be a conscious choice for some of them, their faith may be weaker than that of many converts.

The issue of the potential indifference of some 'born Muslims' to Islamic teachings also surfaces in discussions on *sha'bi* (folk) Islam. Women from Muslim-majority countries and countries where the Muslim minorities are large and well-established, often describe the situation in their communities with unease, expressing discontent about the way that local customs permeate Islamic practices. For example, they echo the normative attitudes that are shown towards the *mawlid* ceremony which is performed in the Yemen (Katz 2008). Sana from India writes:

> There are many groups here, like those who believe in praying in front of tombs called as Dargah{s} and those who call themselves Sunnah al Jamaah, who claim that Qur'an is not for ordinary man to read, it can only be understood by 'Maulana' (...) alone and they read or decipher islam ONLY through mediators! Then there is Qur'aniyoon group [i believe in Mauritaus] who believe ONLY in Qur'aan and say all hadeeth is false [asthagfirullah].

The three groups Sana describes do not belong to the 'mainstream' Islam in that they either worship saints (which is absent from Sunni Islam), do not allow 'lay people' to engage with Islamic sources, or reject the Sunnah of the Prophet. The first and the last practices are especially denounced by the Salafi, who claim that Islam has to be purified of cultural accretions and innovations by adopting the lifestyle of the Companions of the Prophet and the first three generations of Muslims (Ramadan 1999). The second practice goes against the general Islamic principle that there are no mediators between God and the believer.

However, Sana's displeasure is greatest with the scholars whose preaching, in her view, departs from Islamic teachings in spite of being educated at Madina, one of the most important centres of the Islamic world due to its place in the history of Islam.[11] This is especially since they use their degrees from Madina to legitimize traditions that she sees as un-Islamic. Sana condemns the fact that these scholars misguide believers in such an essential issue as Islamic conduct:

> There is one huge university in [her country]. Many scholars who come out of this university [and] go to do PhD at Madina are called 'Madani'[s]. Such people come back here, and inspite of being madani follow and implement their local university misleadings, or precisely follow their forefathers, make islam a family tradition!

Azeezah denounces Islam-related superstitions equally harshly; she reports superstitious beliefs are common among her colleagues, who, for example, link unfortunate incidents with a failure to fulfill the alms (*zakat*) obligation:

> People hardly follow Quran or hadeeth references ... all the knowledge they have is from what their family seniors have asked them to follow. Infact one of the other colleagues said (...), 'we lost some money at home. My mother always says that whenever we loose anything it means that we havent paid zakath for that year in full. My mother always recalculates and if there is any mistake, then we give off, etc' Now where on earth is it written that way? It got so difficult to answer that I once posted a question/request to this group asking for any reference in Quran or Hadeeth.

Azeezah's account indicates that superstitions are strongly rooted in some Muslim communities and their justifications are linked to Islam. Islamic principles get tightly intertwined with folk beliefs that become hard to expound and separate, even for those educated in Islam. It also demonstrates that newsgroups serve a doubly useful function: they are a space where frustrations can be aired with others, and solutions to difficult questions can be found. It may be challenging to find Islamic evidence that a belief or action is against Islam, or does not 'belong' to Islam, as to prove something 'not Islamic' one has to establish that with all Islamic sources and then find counterevidence. Whereas superstitions such as above may, at most, result in one's misguided conduct, there are customs, allegedly Islamic, that may lead to inflicting serious physical harm. Female genital mutilation, or FGM, is, in some contexts, considered a permissible operation. One participant wrote: 'My husband was talking with this brother and he told him that it was sunnah to allow female castration. I know this is not true but i wondered if anyone had anything on hadith and Sunnah about the topic'. This question caused a storm of opinions in the group, as the women were decidedly against the practice, which they referred to as un-Islamic. The majority of women argued similarly to Sawda:

> Circumcision for the female is actually passed over frrom the days of Pharoah in Egypt. It is a tribal custom and it is not at all an islamic practice. Some wish to say that it is just a mere clipping away and is actually better for the female but in actuality the opposite is true. It is painful, can lead to bleeding and shock, infection, death, later on repeated urinary tract infections, and the list goes on, not even mentioning the psychological aspects.

This participant identifies female circumcision as a custom pre-dating the Revelation of Islam that negatively impacts upon female health and psychology. As the practice is common in some of today's African states it has inevitably come into interaction with Islam, and unfortunately for the women, it has received an 'Islamic tag', even though it is also common among Christian tribes (Badawi 1995). Saaba writes:

> i totally agree with u, here in Egypt, there is a strict fatwa that circumcision is haraam and forbidden coz a young girl has died recently,this is like cutting an important part of ur body like ur arm or legs why would anyone take a part that Allah swt has created in u?? adultery is not banned by circumcision, its by the righheous raise up ... plz sisters, lets be more aware of our rights that Allah has given 2 us and never let anyone 2 deprive us from them! BAN CIRCUMCISION.

This posting touches upon one of the arguments presented by advocates of circumcision, that the removal of the clitoris prevents women from lustful behaviour and adultery (Sæverås 2003). As a consequence, the integrity of the Islamic social order is perceived by some as linked to the control over the female body (Pinn 2000). The participant from Egypt mentions that it is a local belief that women in Egypt have an 'unusually large' clitoris that needs 'trimming'. However, she points out, adultery is not prevented by female circumcision practices – only a good upbringing and a pious heart stop one from sinning. As the initiating question shows, its author was interested in evidence with regard to female circumcision, in other words, a verse from the Qur'an or a hadith, which would show what the position of Islam is on the practice. One of the participants provides a hadith which describes an occasion when the Prophet advises a mother to make only a 'small cut' (i.e. only remove the hood of the clitoris) which is better for the girl and her husband.[12] On these grounds, she argues, this kind of female circumcision is *mustahaab* (is neither obligatory nor banned). However, another participant challenges her saying that the even the Ahadith permitting the least-invasive form of female genital mutilation is largely considered as weak:

> *Basheera*: When one looks into the statements of the scholars of hadeeth, however, they will find that quite a number of the most prominent of them, such as Ibn Hajar, al-Bukhari, Abu Dawud, al-

Bayhaqi, ibn-ul-Mundthir, ash-Shawkani, state that they are weak and cannot be relied upon. It is known amongst the scholars of Islam that if a hadeeth is found to be weak and unreliable, it is impermissible that it be used as evidence to establish a ruling in Islam, as all legal rulings in the religion must be verified with authentic, unambiguous proofs.

In addition, the women argue that since circumcision may lead to many complications, it goes against the Qur'anic prescription to do no harm, in harmony with Badawi's (1995) argument. Here, the discussion on female circumcision is embedded in notions of what constitutes sources of Islamic law; the women have different priorities in accepting evidence; one group consider the more general teaching on avoiding harm contained in the Qur'an as the supreme ruling which negates any other evidence that allows any form of female circumcision; a second group look at reliability of the hadith permitting a minor form of circumcision and contend that it is unreliable, thus arguing that it cannot be used to create a law or justify a custom; finally, the third group accept this hadith as permitting female circumcision; however, they do not argue that it is an obligatory act. In these discussions it is not entirely clear why certain women choose to take these quite different positions, that is, in regard to female circumcision and understanding of the hierarchy of Islamic sources. Women arguing against the former on Islamic grounds come from both Muslim-majority and Muslim-minority contexts; also among the defenders of the practice are women who are both likely and unlikely to have been affected by it. This is true also in respect to the approach towards Islamic sources; it would be incorrect to argue that advocates of one position tend to be located either in the West or in a traditionally Muslim context. Understandings of Islamic texts, regardless of their place of origin, have become global in their reach and influence.

One of the women, concluding a discussion on the cultural accretions to Islam writes:

Eiman: It seems too many times that people mistake cultural or traditional views on women's rights with that of Islam. I think that as American Muslimahs we can do a lot to shaken all the misunderstandings that Islam has suffered due to cultural dealings with women.

While her intention may have been to demonstrate what 'pure' Islam is by living it as an *American* Muslim, uninfluenced by presumably Middle Eastern/African/Asian customs, she implies that America is devoid of elements in its culture that are oppressive to women and may be incorporated into the individual behaviour of a believer (and this is not challenged by other participants). However, America, as a relatively new setting for Islam, offers both advantages and difficulties to Muslim women in terms of its culture (Haddad 1997). Eiman also implies that there is one consistent American culture across the country/continent; whereas it would be perhaps more correct to speak about a dominant culture, shaped by white Anglo Saxon protestants, who demand that immigrants, with their 'alien' cultures conform to it (Abbott 2009). They fear that they may be overcome by the plethora of minorities representing a diversity of cultural affiliations, thus implying that they have become a threatened minority in the face of waves of newcomers (Beck and Cronin 2006).

It is perhaps not surprising that in the 'Islam vs. culture' debate, participants concentrate largely on the negative customs that impact Muslim women and not on the positive aspects of culture within Muslim communities, which have enriched the Islamic lifestyle and practices in many ways, including artistically (Brend 1991). As Muslims, the women are likely to be subjected to Islamophobic attacks. These attacks may stem from beliefs which conflate Islamic teachings with some localized customs, such as female genital mutilation or the so called 'honour killings', performed by relatives on a female not conforming to (usually sexuality-related) community norms. Also, as women, they are likely to bear the brunt of these customs, which puts their welfare at risk. Therefore, study of Islamic sources is their best defence in the face of accusations against Islam and attempts to subject them to harmful, un-Islamic practices.

Analytical categories

While frequency of occurrence of certain themes guided the structure of my thesis, I needed different analytic categories to read and interpret the text. Diversity of views suggested the need to identify specific ideological positions which have crystallized during my re-reading of data. These positions have emerged quite clearly from the data, but the process of their identification was more complex. I relied on several types of information: first, categories addressed by other scholars whose work I discussed in Chapter 1; however, I was aware of the fact that because I was working with a different group of women (all of whom defined themselves as religious), my focus would be slightly different. Thus, unlike in Karam's (1998) work I did not identify a secular position in the newsgroups, but instead an anti-feminist position emerged in my research. Eventually I arrived at three categories but some women's postings placed them in two categories. This strongly indicated that placing participants in certain categories may be only tentative and serve analytical purposes, unless they they themselves stated that their views were of a certain kind.

Naming the positions posed another problem, as it was not my intention to ascribe labels to the participants. Careful reading of the data was helpful here, and I realized that the first group of women placed a strong emphasis on equality of gender in Islam and always argued against gender hierarchy. Thus I arrived at the term 'egalitarians'. Another group of women highlighted the significance of tradition, and many of them belonged to a newsgroup whose name included the word tradition in its name. Therefore, I decided to name this position 'traditionalists'. However, there were a large number of participants who seemed to escape this binary. In their postings they advocated unity, friendship, support and an open, searching mind in regard to Islamic issues (egalitarians and traditionalists' views were of a more normative nature). To refer to these participants, I have decided to use the term 'holists' after Badran (2001b), who has identified an unusual form of activism among Yemeni women who have transcended the boundary between secular and religious struggle for the recognition of women's rights; this position highlights the importance of shared interests and joint effort in order to reach a goal, regardless of the framework. Badran argues that the emergence of the holistic position in the Yemen was facilitated by the absence of colonial powers, which prevented western colonialism from being included in the framework of political reference by Yemeni women, whether by affirmation, or by rejection of its values. Thus, in my use holism denotes a holistic approach in accepting the diverse character of Islam, bringing all Islamic discourses to the table (including the 'extreme' ones), and identifying common issues and concerns. I am aware of different uses of the term 'holism', in particular in relation to a political fraction whose aim is establishment of Islamic rule (locally or globally). For instance, Esposito and Voll (1996: 56) write thus about Ayatollah Khomeini: 'His Islamic ideology was holistic, regarding Islam as a total and complete way of life that provided guidance for social and political life'. In this sense, holism means applying Islam to regulate all aspects of human existence. However, often a very specific understanding of Islam is used to create a basis for such regulation, which prevents sustained pluralism of views within the Islamic framework. This differentiates the latter usage of the concept of holism from the former (mine). The three identified positions constitute an analytic framework for the subsequent chapters. However, I should note here that this book looks beyond the differences, and how these can lead to divisions within online communities, and emphasizes the ways in which traditionalists, egalitarians, and holists attempt to engage in a common debate and understand each other's views.

In this chapter, participants' views on have been analysed through an examination of intersecting themes of Islamic education and Islamic and cultural practices. On the continuum that these views form, it is possible to identify three positions which are defined by: women's attitudes to the type of preferred engagement with Islamic sources; accepted Islamic sources; and finally, their views on Islamic principles and the actual practices of believers. In spite of sometimes considerable differences in opinions, participants do not ignore each other. Although discussions may be heated, women actively engage with each other's views, and, from time to time, come to an agreement. This may be a result of the specificity of the online environment, which brings together women who otherwise would not have had a chance to interact whether due to their geographical location or their epistemological position. Sometimes women express astonishment at encountering entirely different views from their own but the chance of engaging with such views can be interpreted as an advancement of women's sisterhood – women come out of their own localized environments and face others, who think differently.

Traditionalists invoke Qur'anic verses and Ahadith that grant men more power in the family and society, and argue that they were revealed due to women's attributes which are more useful in the home sphere, referring to tenderness, mildness, as well as forgetfulness, and a less analytical mind. In terms of interpretation of the sources, traditionalists recommend engagement with readings of established Islamic scholars, and warn that individual interpretation may lead to an erroneous understanding of Islam. In contrast to other groups, traditionalists do not see a discrepancy between Islamic scripture and general Muslim practices. What other Muslim contest as patriarchal interpretations and cultural influence, they see as legitimate Islamic law. Traditionalists argue that 'alternative' readings dilute the word of God, and that while living a life according to Islamic standards may be at times difficult it should be understood as a test. This position is probably most misconstrued by both other Muslims and non-Muslims alike. However, the perception of a 'conservative' Muslim woman as silent and oppressed is based on using a specific system of values, which promotes personal independence, open choice and power. In fact, these women choose this traditional life path; it is not forced on them. They are willing to give up some things that are generally understood as personal rights in order to gain acceptance in the eyes of God, which is, to them, the highest reward. As Franks (2001: 187) found, 'because they [traditionalist respondents] do not hanker after the autonomous model of empowerment they find the connectedness which they gain from being part of a believing community empowering'. Karim (2008: 181) argues that women for whom piety is the only motivation represent 'forms of women's agency that resonate with Islamic feminist practice' because they make their own choices and believe that they have the right to act according to their own convictions. They often mention that life in this *dunya* (world) is just a test before the afterlife, which can be either *Jannah* (Paradise) or Hellfire. Therefore, mundane matters are of consequence only as long as they impact on one's Islamic conduct. One participant writes: 'remember this life is just an illusion and we have to realize that we go through tests all our life and we shouldnt lose our soul for a problem in this life'.

A mode of engagement with Islamic sources recommended by egalitarians is the individual mode; although they do not reject scholars altogether, they argue that the Qur'an does not prescribe any intermediaries between God and believers. Participants who support this position carefully delineate between Islam and local customs of Muslim communities; they advocate an active participation in Islamic education in order to explode the myth that Islam is an intrinsically patriarchal religion. It is their view that patriarchy is ubiquitous across the world and Islam, like other religion, has been 'hijacked' by males in order to subdue women through the construction of biased readings, and the passing off of unIslamic misogynistic practices as Islamic.

Echoing Badawi (1995), holists hold that genders in Islam are not competitive but co-operative and complementary. Like women representing the egalitarian position, they conduct individual readings of Islamic sources. They point out that Islam gives them many rights that are still not enjoyed by non-Muslim women, such as the right to keep all their money and not contribute to the household expenses; moreover, the husband has to maintain his wife in the style to which she was accustomed before marriage; Muslim women also have the right to be paid for the suckling of their babies (Afshar 1998). In return, they agree to fulfil the household duties, although they expect their husbands to help out, in the spirit of Prophet Muhammad's Sunnah. Islamic education is also one of their priorities, as it allows them to reclaim Islamic rights and defend Islam whenever it is under attack.

The participants also represent variant views on the role of culture, in the sense of traditions, customs, and sometimes specific prejudices, in the life of a believer. Depending on their position, they define Islam in different ways, and. consequently, they differently understand what is unIslamic. Those who see Islam as a religion based on gender hierarchy are more comfortable with the existence of contexts where women's access to public facilities such as education or mosques is limited. They accept justifications of those limitations that are derived from traditional interpretations of Islamic sources. Other women, in particular supporters of the Salafi movement, are against certain customs related to practising Islam which have emerged in varied cultural contexts, and argue for a purification of religion, redefining it solely on the basis of the Quran and the Sunnah. Among the participants, there is a deep suspicion of 'culture', as many born Muslim women interpret their negative experiences with members of Muslim communities as resulting from a lack of the latter's correct Islamic education and indifference to the true message of Islam. Finally, there are egalitarians who concentrate on the gendered aspect of 'culture', and reject interpretations highlighting the need for different treatment of genders. They argue that readings of Islamic sources are shaped by cultural contexts their authors grew up in. In other words, whereas the Qur'an is complete and perfect, its interpretations will always remain products of the human mind. Consequently, they argue that negating 'culture' as a whole is an illusion.

Notes

1 Female companions of Prophet Muhammad.
2 Salafis are also known as Wahhabis, after the founder of the movement, Muhammad abd Al-Wahhab (1703–92) (Nanji and Nanji 2008).
3 It is impossible to obtain exact statistics, but according to a poll kindly organized by a moderator of one newsgroup, out of 37 women who took part in it, 60 per cent lived in the United States, 20 per cent in Europe, and 20 per cent in Muslim-majority countries, mostly Egypt, Morocco,

Pakistan, and Bangladesh.

4 See Sahih Muslim, *Book* 35, Number 6518. Throughout the book I refer to translations of Ahadith collections published online by the Center for Muslim-Jewish Engagement, University of South California (http://www.usc.edu/schools/college/crcc/engagement/resources/texts/muslim/hadith/ accessed 1 April 2011).

5 It should be noted that while Sunni Muslims revere Aisha, Shi'a Muslims consider Fatima, the Prophet's daugter, as a female role model in Islam; they do not respect Aisha and argue that she was "more concerned with securing the caliphate for her father, Abu Bakr, than with transmitting the teachings of Islam in Muhammad's spirit" (Hyder, 2006: 75).

6 *Haafitha* of Qur'an – somebody who memorized the Qur'an.

7 This participant may be referring to the Qur'anic verse 4:59 which reads: "O you who believe! Obey Allaah and obey the Messenger, and those of you who are in authority".

8 Badawi (1995) differentiates between gender equality and equity in order to avoid criticisms that equality means 'absolute sameness' in relation to rights and responsibilities.

9 *Saheeh/sahih* means reliable, authentic (Farooq, 2006: 1), as opposed to weak Ahadith.

10 Although my Internet search of a number of news outlets, including Al-Jazeera and Afghan News, did not return any information specifically on the violence of Allied troops against Afghan women, it revealed extensive information on the "allegation of sexual abuse" by UN personnel in Somalia, Congo, Bosnia, Kosovo, Cambodia, East Timor and West Africa. It was reported that in Bosnia and Kosovo, a sex industry, based on trafficked women, was created in order to serve the stationed NATO forces (War Resisters International, http://www.wri-irg.org/node/6716 accessed on 27 June 2009). Considering this, one cannot dismiss participant A17's accusation as unprecedented.

11 Madina is the city to which Prophet Muhammad migrated in 622 and from where he united the Arab tribes. It is the place of the Prophet's burial and the second holiest city in Islam (Armstrong 2006).

12 See Sunan Abu Dawud, *Book* 41, Number 5251. See also Malik's Muwatta, *Book* 2, Numbers 2.19.73, 2.19.74, 2.19.75, 2.19.76, and 2.19.77.

3   Marriage, sexuality and polygamy

In this chapter I discuss a selection of women's postings about their personal lives. It is important to consider the institution of marriage because in Islam it is the only legitimate site for exploring and enjoying one's sexuality (Sachedina 1990). I also look at women's expectations regarding their husbands and their interpretation of circumstances which make divorce possible. Views on sexuality are explored, as they closely intertwine with concepts of marriage. Discussions on marriage are also the context for women's explorations of issues of hierarchy, power, control, rights and responsibilities in the fourth of my themes: the polygamous marriage. Views that emerge in all these explorations feed back into the three previously identified categories of women's perceptions of gender relations in Islam.

Marriage

Marriage is a central institution in Islam for facilitating religious and social life (Sherif 1999). It is recommended to every Muslim who can afford it, because it serves two important functions: it connects two human beings who were originally created 'for each other', and it allows procreation (Sachedina 1990). The Qur'an reads: 'And God has created for you consorts (in marriage) from amongst yourselves, and through your consorts He created children and grandchildren for you, and provided you of His bounty. Will they then believe in vain things and be ungrateful to God's favours'(16: 72). Barlas (2006) argues that marriage in Islam is located at the boundary between private and public, due to its contractual nature, however, she also claims that the Qur'an does not make distinctions between the public and the private.

Marriage-related debates emerge when women share marital problems on the forum – other women come up with advice on how to improve the situation based on their own idea of a perfect marriage. One exchange began when Azza asked for advice how to communicate with her husband successfully and attain happiness in her marriage: 'my problem is that my husband always expects me to be in a good mood ... Now we aren't talking and he has said enough that I don't want to talk and I have said enough that he doesn't want to talk'. The women who responded can be seen to represent different points of view with regard to the enhancement of Azza's marriage.

Naima, who is a traditionalist, tries to help Azza and recalls a hadith which says that it is the role of the wife to seek reconciliation between spouses before the day ends, which is based on hadith in Sahih Al-Bukhari:[1] 'If a husband calls his wife to his bed and she refuses and causes him to sleep in anger, the angels will curse her till morning'. She emphasizes that the wife has to be compliant with her husband's wishes and never seek satisfaction by countering her husband's arguments:

If you want to attain Allah's pleasure, and if you want to attain a peaceful marriage you MUST learn to sacrifice having the last say. From your message it sounds like your husband wasn't being harsh or unfair, he was merely behaving the way any husband would. Remember that if your husband goes to sleep while he is angry with you, the Angels curse you til the morning.

Naima's argument is located within the traditionalist discourse, which sees women's domestic activities as fulfilment of a responsibility prescribed by God. Wadud (2000) defines this type of traditionalist perspective as conservative; it constructs a woman as dependent on the male relatives in her household, who establish her legitimacy. Gender roles shape not only the kind of occupation a spouse may have, but also a hierarchy in which the husband is the family leader. This view is based on a specific reading of the Qur'anic verse 2:228 which in some translations and interpretations reads that men have 'a degree over' women.[2] However, the same verse reads that 'women have similar rights over men as men have over women'. Traditionalists stress that a wife should not abuse her rights over her husband (they acknowledge that a wife has them) and try to take over the control in the relationship, which, in the opinion of traditionalists characterizes western feminism. Lamya states that deliberations of modernist Islamic scholars (she mentions Jamal Badawi) on women's rights in marriage should not be uncritically accepted, as they are likely to dress up western concepts as Islamic rights:

Just because we can claim rights on our husbands similar to the rights they can claim on us, this doesn't mean we can jump on the Women's Liberation band wagon and rule our husbands or behave in a domineering fashion, dragging them through the mud for every little personality conflict or overly enthusiastic rule on us.

This perspective is defined by Wadud (2000) as reactionary. Lamya criticizes western feminism which she perceives as responsible for the breakdown of marriage and family; in a wider context, reactionary traditionalists challenge dominant western discourses on Islam as an 'oppressive religion' and create their own discourse to defend the 'name of Islam' by negating the position of women in the West, contradicting the achievements of secular feminism, and portraying 'western values' as incompatible with, and harmful to Islam. It is argued by feminist Muslim scholars that in a situation where opposition to the West and preservation of what is considered 'Muslim identity', is conducted at all costs, when the costs entail ignoring the spirit of the primary sources of Islam (which is, from gender scholarship's perspective, intrinsically egalitarian), the opposition ceases to be Islamic (Wadud 2000).

Barlas (2006) recommends Wadud's reading of verse 4:34 which is used by traditionalists to justify the right of husbands to beat their disobedient wives and to require obedience from them in marital affairs. Wadud's reading of the term *qanitat* (obedience) is that it refers to a 'moral attitude of obedience on the part of both women and men to God' (2006: 187). In a similar vein, Abugideiri (2001: 8) argues that it was a 'pick and choose' method by modern *fiqh* judges who established the rule of male dominance in marriage, leading to the popular belief that wife beating is allowed in Islam.

Aasiya, who is an egalitarian, similarly disagrees with the notion of wifely obedience advocated by traditionalists and argues that men are likely to abuse their wives' goodwill and effort to please God. Aasiya criticizes the understanding of marital obedience as full, unquestioning compliance. Although she makes a disclaimer that she does not think that all men are likely to exploit their wives, she states that many men support patriarchy and misogyny in marriage:

I believe that when men are allowed to believe that they are superior, and that women must 'obey' them in the same manner that a child obeys a parent; it encourages them to abuse their 'power'. I believe it encourages them to abuse their wives. This is not a blanket observation of all men. But, unfortunately, there are too many men who fit into this ideology.

Aasiya identifies the source of the problem as occurring in traditional gender roles, challenging the traditionalist perception of gender hierarchy that places men above women. By observing that men are *allowed* to believe in their superiority, she highlights society's consent to this process and its active role in the consolidation of patriarchy through the employment of male-focused patterns and objectives in the education of children. Aasiya's posting is a challenge to patriarchy; she sees gender inequality as abuse. Aasiya situates her discourse in the Islamic framework: 'Nowhere in the Qur'an does Allah state or imply that women are inferior and/or subservient to men. If this foolishness is not in the Qur'an, it's automatically not in the Sunnah of Prophet Muhammad (Allah's Peace be upon him)'. This statement suggests that, like Wadud (1999) and Barlas (2006), Aasiya does not interpret verse 2:228 as establishing gender hierarchy. Moreover, she argues that because the Qur'an, the central Islamic source, does not introduce gender hierarchy, it is impossible that the principles of the Sunnah, next in the Islamic source hierarchy, would go against the gender ideology of the Qur'an. This was the premise of Fatima Mernissi (in Ouedghiri 2002: 47), when she challenged the 'misogynistic hadith' reported by Abu Bakr who claimed that the Prophet stated, 'those who entrust their affairs to a woman will never know prosperity'.[3] Mernissi found that there were many suggestive events which preceeded the revealing of this hadith and indicated that it was likely to have been fabricated; she asserted that it was but one example of an occasion when the Prophet's words were made subject to fraudulence.

In the discussions on the preferred type of marriage, Hana and Jameela take the holistic position and gently point out that it is in the interest of all women to be happy Muslim wives. They emphasize that paths to happiness are different for everybody and highlight such qualities of marriage as mutuality (advocating 'sameness' of rights would imply influence of radical western feminism, which Hana wants to avoid), equal importance, respect, care and acceptance of a spouse's imperfections. Hana refers back to verse 2: 187 of the Qur'an which underscores the mutual rights and responsibilities of spouses, while Jameela points out that marriage is not a single moment in time, but a process which has to be sustained by appropriate efforts of both spouses to make it work. Importantly, Jameela asks other women to be less 'politically inclined' and confrontational, and suggests that work for the benefit of one's marriage is in the interest of everybody.

> *Hana*: One of the most beautiful descriptions of the relationship between a husband and a wife is the aya[4] that says that the wife and the husband are garments for each other. I read that aya, and I understand that there is MUTUALITY in it. I understand that there is EQUALITY in it. When I say, 'equality', I don't mean identicalness. I mean I believe it affirms that men and women are of equal value, and they are equally important in a marriage. We must respect each other, we must care for each other. This is what I believe Allah intends for married people.

> *Jameela*: Dear sisters, all i wanted to say is don't get politically inclined, or take a couple of views and make it a vantage point, or suffer over it in a state of oppression. Life is short, days are annoyingly passing like moments. take it easy, or try to, and put on your thinking hats and start playing to win the marriage game. After all, Marriage is not the end but the begining of a main challenge. Marriage is beautiful. Just teh (sic) way how we want to see it – Half full? Half empty?

These two quotes justify the need to take the middle ground in a variety of different ways. Hana employs the way of religious discourse, locating her argument within Qur'anic principles which should guide the spouses' behaviour. Through this, her posting gains a higher degree of legitimacy in the online discussion. Jameela, on the other hand, takes a 'practical' approach, and appeals to women's 'down to earth' style of thinking. She describes marriage as a challenge but also a process, which can be shaped and interpreted by the women involved; by writing this, she is trying to motivate other women to stop fruitless debates and engage in the action of 'winning the marriage game'. Jameela does not, in this post, relate to men, even though the thread is about marriage – she focuses on women and their choices to which they have a full right.

Discussions on marriage often involve the subject of partner choice. Positions on gender relations determine who the women think has the right to choose the marriage partner: the family or the person involved. The marrying age is a related theme which is also debated. The following conversation developed between four participants who took the traditionalist position; they stated that girls should be married off by their parents early on in their lives. This view stems from the traditionalist premise that women are defined through their relationship with men, and once a girl is physically mature, she can be made dependent upon her husband, which from then on, socially and economically shapes her identity (Afshar 1985).

> *Huda*: I read about the parents involvement in marrying their daughters, When the daughter reachs a mature age (like 14), it is the duty of her parents and/or male relatives to find her a suitable husband.
>
> *Iman*: i can say abt me that i hate to search and wud love seeing my father searching instead inshAllah.But when he doesnt finds around and ask to take help of matrimonial sites Alhamdulillah. ppl r more concerned abt telling their salary rather telling abt deen allahu alam.
>
> *Lateefah*: but the problem with the girls in this society now, especially the ones from this generation who are of age is lack of self control and deen. most sisters i know who should be married and out of shytans temptation are 'not ready' for marraige. they want to look around and take they're time.i mean after all 'there are plenty of fish in the sea lol.[5]
>
> *Rabeea*: Yeah, that's somewhat the case in Pakistan as well, since the western ideology and culture has stepped in. But you know, there's another story too. There are girls here who would want to get married in their teens but their parents are not ready, forcing them to complete their studies first. I guess there's no moderation here.

Matchmaking is seen by traditionalists as the elders' responsibility. As Haddad *et al.* (2006: 89) state, 'in traditional Islamic countries marriage involves more than two people', as the decision to marry is not only up to the couple themselves. Traditionalists hold that because young women often act upon impulse and the western ideal of romantic love, it is recommended that a girl's parents chose her husband. This ensures that the man she marries possesses the essential qualities of a good Muslim husband, as the parents are in a better position to make a judgement of the man's character than the girl. They are more likely to select someone on the basis of piety rather than looks, charm or wealth. However, some traditionalist women complain that their families do not fulfill their duty in this respect. Iman expresses her disappointment in relation to her father's lack of effort in finding her a good husband.

She dismisses her father's suggestion that she use Internet matchmaking websites; her main concern is the spouses's piety, Islamic education and good character, whereas, in her view, men looking for brides online tend to emphasize their wealth or good looks, which makes them undesirable. Bunt (2009: 104–12) in his discussion of Muslim matrimonial websites states that online matchmaking is becoming increasingly acceptable, as it is grounded in 'pragmatic religious and cultural norms'. In some contexts it may reinforce traditional practices such as arrangement of marriage by the family, which may now be performed via the Internet, but in others it may 'transcend cultural restrictions and religious values'.

Malhotra (1991) argues that early arranged marriages signal an orientation toward traditional family roles. Traditionalists see marriage as beneficial for women, therefore Huda recommends it for girls of 14 and older, although it is not clear from the discussion why this age limit is mentioned, especially as the lower commonly known marriage age limit is 9 years old for girls, which reflects the age of Ai'sha at the time her marriage was consummated by the Prophet (Ahmed 1992). It is seen as a means of prevention of zina (sexual sins) from an early age, that is, containing bodily needs in the legal institution of marriage, as opposed to encouraging illegal sex outside of marriage. Some traditionalists argue that young women put marriage off because they are tempted by *Shaytan* (the devil) to enjoy life as single women, which is a violation of God's wish.

The question of the 'individualistic' western culture arises as traditionalist women discuss the reasons why the tradition of marrying young is relatively unpopular among Muslims. Rabeea from Pakistan sees the source of women's lack of the wish to marry embedded in the westernization of both the girls and the parents, who may insist that their daughters complete their education beforehand. Traditionalists see such a wish as misguided and sinful. It is associated with lack of faith and, in girls, lack of self control, a quality which is seen as integral to feminine submission. It is worth noting that it is only secular, university education that is seen as an obstacle to marrying, women's right to an Islamic education is not questioned. Indeed, it is perceived as a believer's duty, compatible with her/his gender roles. Heaton's study (2003: 5) confirms this link between a traditional perspective and the disapproval of women's non-familial roles: 'Family environments which socialize women toward being wives and mothers, also discourage orientation toward careers … As a result, daughters would receive less financial support even if they wanted to continue their schooling'.

Sabeera joins this conversation and mentions her American nationality, followed by an account of her arranged marriage, as recommended by traditionalists:

> I am an American woman who is now married to a man chosen for me by my mother and brother in law. I agreed to marry him because my mother felt he was a good choice. I wasn't even in love with him when I agreed to marry him. Thank God love did come later. I have never known this level of happiness with anyone. My mother is an American convert to Islam ... is usually right about people and I know that I can trust her judgment.

By mentioning being an American and a pious Muslim almost in one breath, she suggests that one can be an American Muslim who follows Islamic principles (which are, in this case, obedience and trust in parents' choices), even when these principles are unpopular or perceived by other Muslims as incompatible with the western values of freedom and independence of the individual.[6] By claiming her Americanness, Sabeera negotiates her American Muslim identity, which has become particularly complex after 9/11 and the 'war on terror' that followed (Karim 2008).

Marriage is seen by traditionalists as an end of personal independence and the beginning of life as a unit, with the husband in charge, and with obedience emerging out of love, not coercion. Ada writes: 'We as women do have to make some sacrifices [in marriage] as well, especially if you are used to be an independent women as i was'. Some women who represent the traditionalist position do not have the option of marriage arranged by family, for instance they are converts, and they are instead forced to make marriage-related enquiries themselves. Unable to rely on family advice, they are very careful in their choice of spouse; aware that in case of marital discord they do not have relatives to turn to, they prefer to turn down uncertain candidates. For example, Gazala writes on the forum that she thanks all women who wished her well on her upcoming marriage (the wishes of happiness formed an entire thread), but after conversations with her fianceé, rather than risk a later divorce, which is a thing hated by God, she decided not to marry, employing her agency for personal and religious reasons.

Egalitarians do not see marriage as absolutely compulsory for Muslim women, in line with feminist Muslim scholars' argument (Hassan 2000). They also disagree with the concept of early marriage as advocated by traditionalists, and point to potential problems linked to arranged marriages. Early marriage, in their view, may result in a union of immature young people who do not stand a chance of forming a successful relationship. According to Aasiya, a special effort must be made to bring up male children in the spirit of gender equality, educate them and prepare for marriage rather than marry them off too early:

> Children must be prepared for future marriage. Like females, male children must also be nurtured and given sound, positive guidance and direction from loving, caring, Allah-conscious mothers and fathers. Boys must never be brought up to think that being male means belonging to the 'chosen gender', thus looking at girls as being inferior to them just for being female. If they grow up to be men with this perverted thinking, they will perceive themselves as having some special, God-like powers to lord over women, wives in particular. If any man was unfortunately taught this during his childhood, he must absolutely debunk it long before he even thinks about courtship and marriage.

This argument is also located in the Islamic framework. Aasiya, by using the expression 'as having some special, God-like powers' challenges the discourse which grants men, in Barlas's (2006: 15) words, perceived 'sexual partisanship' with God through the engenderment of God as Father (male). Barlas dismantles this belief by reminding her readers of the principle that God is 'Incomparable, hence Unrepresentable, especially in antropomorphic terms' (2006: 15). Aasiya again focuses on the process of education, vesting in it a hope that boys can be taught to become men who implement in their lives the egalitarian message of Islam. Otherwise, in Aasiya's view, their marriages cannot be successful.

In addition, for girls, an early marriage often means an early pregnancy and 'usually an end to a woman's educational opportunities' (Fatimah) which is confirmed by studies on the relationship between early marriage and socioeconomic and familial status (Heaton 2003). Arranged marriage, according to egalitarians, is allowed only if the girl expresses acceptance of the potential husband – however, egalitarians emphasize that forced marriages, arranged by parents without their daughter's consent, are invalid. They back this view with two Ahadith; the first one is a story of a woman who went to the Prophet and said that she was married by her parents to a man she despised, and the

Prophet anulled her marriage;[7] in the second one the Prophet is reported to have said that consent in marriage has to be obtained both from a previously married woman and a virgin.[8] Egalitarians also stress that forced marriages constitute woman abuse, which should be condemned by Muslim communities.

The qualities of a good husband are a topic which attracts many contributors. Women dispute what desired and undesired traits are, and consider which of the undesired traits may lead to divorce by the woman. Afrah, an American traditionalist convert, reports that she included a stipulation that her husband was to be a properly practising Muslim and that he would assist her in her Islamic education as she attempted to improve her deen in the marriage. This reveals her expectations about her husband's qualities:

> My husband taught me to read the quran within one month after we were married, so I put that to use and started to read more, although i had no idea of what I was readin loool. (mind ya he had to teach me cause that was one of the conditions I stipulated in our marriage contract looool that and that he HAD to pray 5 times a day or divorce) loooool mind ya, you can divorce on that score anyways … but I felt better that it was on paper to back me up LOOOOOOL

Afrah is known in the newsgroups as one of the strictest members and one of the best authorities on Islamic sources. In her posting she writes about the beginning of her marriage, which took place soon after her conversion. Although she was new both to Islam and to marriage, her story reveals a strong personality and conviction: she had a marriage contract (which she advocates to other women in the newsgroup as it is an Islamic right that gives her a great sense of security), and in the contract she set very specific conditions, in that her husband had to teach her to read the Qur'an (presumably, in Arabic as her husband is an Arab), and pray five times a day, under the threat of divorce. This indicates the great value she attached to the piety of her spouse.

Alaia praises her husband for being understanding and gentle to her when she experienced post-natal depression and stopped praying, but to her it also matters a lot that he prays regularly. In that sense, he has set a good example to her and the children without using any coercion or threats:

> *Alaia*: I used to be a devout prayer. After marriage and during pregnancy things went too hard and in my depression I also stopped praying. My husband prays 5 times a day. But he never objected to me. Sometimes he would remind me gently but not forced anything.

Alaia, a wife in a traditional household, describes a more lenient attitude to the unobservance of Islamic teachings by her spouse. Her account recalls his gentle perseverance in reminding about the times of prayer and, ultimately, of her return to prayer observance. The example of Alaia's marriage indicates that a husband in a traditional household may be merciful and quiet-tempered in his dealings in his wife; it provides a counterbalance to the stereotype of a violent husband in a family which is male-led and works according to traditional gender norms (Ayyub 2000).

These postings, indicating that Afrah and Alaia have pious and gentle husbands, caused unrest among other participants, both traditionalist (e.g. Saida) and egalitarian (e.g. Muna), as they began posting their reflections on some husbands' behaviours which obviously were far from their expectations of how a 'good Muslim husband' should act:

> *Saida*: My husband is not praying, not going to jumah, nor reading the holy book and doesn't seem to want to return to the way he was before. I am very seriously thinking he is not going to return to the life that is best. I am concerned about the affects on the children. My husband is not a good model for them because he doesn't pray … On the one hand I think I should separate from my husband for some time. Try to get myself nearer to the muslim community so my children will see more people like myself.
> *Muna*: There is a REASON why, Divorce wasn't made haram … and that is because, Allah doesn't want you to be oppressed, or feel like you've been jailed and live a distasteful life. Abusive men in most cases remain abusive throughout their lives. They do change somewhat in most cases … BUT IS THAT ENOUGH TO RAISE A GREAT MUSLIM CHILD??? Specially if you aren't able to be your best self either?

This exchange indicates that although participants (regardless of their position) may deem marriage as very important, they allow the possibility of a divorce in certain cases, in contrast to Catholic marriages, which cannot be revoked. In contrast, Saida's husband's behaviour (not praying and drinking alcohol) is considered an offense against God and family. As he does not seem to want to change, she considers separation from him for the sake of the children, who, in her view, should grow up under an Islamic influence. Muna articulates many women's thoughts very precisely, advocating divorce from him, suggesting that if the children have to grow up in an unIslamic environment, they are in danger of losing their faith. While divorce is the permissible action most disliked by Allah,[9] some situations merit resorting to it and in her view, this is such a case.

Traditionalists' conversations focus on the separation from Islam as the main failure of husbands. They expect husbands to be providers, but mainly they wish to see them as Muslim role models for both themselves and their children. These debates illustrate traditionalist women's determination to live a life which is in accordance with their understanding of piety. As long as the husband fits into this concept and demonstrates by his piety and actions that he is worthy of respect, he is given it. However, if he deviates from the Islamic path or hinders the wife's Islamic activities, he is likely to be divorced. Such an approach suggests that marriage is central to traditionalist women as long as it facilitates the fulfilment of God's wishes. Women use their own judgement in assessing the qualities of their own marriages, and this comes across as a sign of high self-worth and empowerment. This attitude also characterized the life of Zeinab al-Ghazali, a conservative Muslim activist in Egypt who divorced her husband when he attempted to stop her from participating in Islamic organizations (Hijab 1988).

Looking after one's husband and children are seen as the core of a woman's domestic role; however, participants' views are sometimes 'tokenistic' on this subject, in other words, it is clear that although they know what is required from them (in terms of the traditionalist interpretation of Islam), they act differently, either out of choice or need (Franks 2001). Alimah writes that 'Woman is the home manager, above all', but then goes on to analyse how it is more difficult for her to bear the double burden of housework and work outside the home. It is clear that although many women would prefer to adhere to traditional rulings, for example that women should not mix with non-mahram males, necessity forces them to negotiate theory and practice.

Traditionalists' views on marriage are expressed in great detail; most participants in this category accept and affirm strict hierarchy in the family: first, obedience is due to God, then to the husband, as long as the husband does not hinder the wife's religious responsibilities. Children

owe obedience to their parents. Women's role as mothers is fundamental
to the family, and many women see a source of empowerment in
taking this role. In addition, in many traditional families the status of
women rises once they give birth to male children (Oni 1996; Nauck
and Klaus 2005). Traditionalists' views on motherhood affirm their role
as a mother, which in their view has also religious importance. Hanfa
comments: 'I mean, we are given the most important task of our live ...
and that is RAISING OUR UMMAH !!!!'. Women's concern to raise
good Muslim children may also benefit the women themselves. The
interests of her children is one of the most common reasons given when
a woman ponders on the forum whether or not she should leave an
abusive husband. Traditionalists argue that it is impossible to raise a
healthy child in an abusive environment, and importantly, they point
out that 'Allah helps those who help themselves' which suggests that
they are aware of their right to actively shape their lives according to
the Creator's design.

In discussions on marriage, egalitarians see the main problem rooted
in the social construct which promotes men's dominance in marriage,
just as Muslim feminists argue that patriarchy is embedded in traditions
and customs (Hassan 2001; Barlas 2006). Aasiya argues that the Islamic
ideal of male protection for women, expressed in verse 2:228, has been
abused and transformed into dominance, possessiveness and control
in the household; and that men's duty to provide financially for their
families has been used as a justification to put men on the 'family
pedestal'. Her further observation is that raising male children in the
way that suggests that they have 'God-like' powers, is a violation of the
Islamic doctrine of *Tawhid*, based on the belief that there is only one
God and Muslims' main allegiance is to God, not any humans. This is
also acknowledged by traditionalists, however, they intepret it in such a
way that does not put Tawhid in conflict with the gender hierarchy. This
doctrine is also considered by Barlas (2006) as one of the reasons why
Islam is not, in its divine design, a patriarchal religion.

Women representing the holistic category have a practical approach
to Islamic injunctions and as they seem to be at peace with their
understandings of Islam within the wider Muslim community, they
take the role of providing support within the newsgroups to those who
explicitly express a request for marital advice, echoing the findings of
Bastani (2001) about emotional support in Muslim women's online
groups. Advice from one's Muslim sisterhood is taken seriously,

especially that they often offer prayer (du'a) on behalf of the one who needs support. Many women admit that the newsgroup is the only place where they feel comfortable talking about their problems, as non-Muslim counsellors do not understand Islamic norms and values, therefore their advice is not best suited for Muslim women. As some participants are also trained counsellors, they often offer professional advice to those who come to the forum with troubles. Emotional support is therefore strengthened by practical advice based on Islamic principles. Islamic education enables women to discern whether their rights are upheld or infringed upon in their marriages. In cases when a participant does not have sufficient knowledge on a matter, she may consult her sisters, who usually put a lot of effort into ensuring that an answer is found, either by researching the issue on their own or referring to a scholar. Alma writes thus in response to a woman who asked if her divorce was valid: 'First sister, I would be sure to look into your rights and obligations in regards to marriage and divorce. Inshallah, it would be beneficial to know all of your rights as a married woman to protect yourself from harm'. After that she goes on to provide an Islamic interpretation of the situation and give her suggestions about the course of action. Such an approach is very helpful, for as Bunt writes (2000: 126): 'individuals might apply aspects of the phenomena presented online in order to enhance their religious lives or knowledge'. It is likely that information obtained in the newsgroups is used in the offline world.

A comment later added later to the discussion on divorce by Afrah indicates the holistic position, which shows that although in most of her statements she speaks in line with strict traditionalist views (emphasising a wife's obedience and sacrifice), when it comes to wife mistreatment that borders on abuse, she does not enforce any opinions on the woman involved:

I believe that every situation is different. One cannot judge the hearts of all people. Some are genuine sorry for their hurtings and the others absolutely need to be put out of their misery. To look upon the matter of just leave and get out should be weighed very seriously and things should be consulted with high precaution and have solutions prescribed. If then things do not improve, then do your best to escape. Allah swt does test us in ways we think are so wrong for us, but yet, the outcome are rewards if we pass the test. Allah swt knows best.

Her premise is that in such a serious situation nobody has the right to tell the victim of violence what to do, instead she has to come to a decision herself. Whatever the victim's decision is (to leave or to stay), it should be accepted as a legitimate decision. Afrah makes the point that divorce should not be dictated, yet is still a valid option. She sees a difficult situation like this as a test from God, who however does not put soul under a 'burden heavier than it can bear' (Qur'an 2: 286). This posting suggests that women in the newsgroups have relatively fluid views, which do not constitute static categories; many women move between traditionalist, holistic and egalitarian stances, depending on the topic of conversation.

Sexuality

Acknowledgement of women's sexuality in Islam is a feature of their religion much appreciated by Muslim women in the newsgroups. In contrast to Christianity, in Islam, female sexuality is considered 'active', rather than 'passive' (Gerami 1995: 5). Mernissi (2001) argues that Islam's view of female sexuality is that of a powerful force. Sexuality is seen not only as an element of the procreative function, but also as a sphere of life to be enjoyed by both spouses (Arnfred 2003). However, the theme of women's sexual pleasure is but one in a very complex discourse of female body politics in Islam. This discourse includes other themes such as safeguarding women's modesty (and men's honour) through segregation; control of women's sexuality through body part removal (e.g. female genital mutilation), and female sexuality as a threat to men's honour (Rashid 2003). These phenomena have been discussed in the literature as characteristic of some cultures where Islam is predominant (Badawi 1995). Also, it is characteristic of Islam (and in this it is similar to other monotheistic mainstream religions) that sexuality is celebrated only within marriage, whereas outside of marriage, sexual relations are considered *zina* (fornication, unlawful, punishable) (Husni and Newman 2007). In spite of this, young adults in Muslim majority contexts, especially from middle and upper classes, do engage in premarital sex (Hooshmand 2003).

Discussions on sexuality are a part of a complex debate on gender relations and marriage. Participants in the discussions, with assistance from Islamic sources, explore the topic of sexuality in a quest to better understand what their rights and responsibilities are. Their views may considerably differ, as in the case of other topics discussed so far. In this analysis I look at a debate on sexual rights and responsibilities in Islam that resulted in the construction of some complex arguments in support of opposing viewpoints, as well as in the attempts of the holists to find a middle ground. Nadja, a traditionalist, elaborates on the conjugal sexual duties of both spouses in Islam, but she is challenged by Aasiya, an egalitarian, who in turn is challenged by another traditionalist, Hawwa:

> *Nadja*: In the matter of sexual rights, we all know that Qur'an tells us that we have rights on them similar to what they have on us. The similarity is in the fact that they must fulfill our needs at least once in a four month period. We, on the other hand, must fulfill their needs at any moment they require us, as long as the means are halal (in private, not during menses, not during the fast of Ramadhan and not anal).

> *Aasiya*: No disrespect to you, dear sister, but to me, this sounds like you're implying that the husband's libido takes front-and-center in a marriage simply because he's the man. I just don't buy that for one minute.

> *Hawwa*: Sis, i am against your opinion whatever you wanted to explain about the relationship for marraige. But sis as far as I know and with the Knowledge of Allah who give to me, marriage is uncomplete without sexual relationship. I have husband before but he died for almost 6 years now ... But you know we dont make any bad arguments or war between me and my late husband ... Sis i know that man is verry (sic) eager specially in bed, and yes thier libido is greater than women ... We women can be patient without man in our life but most man can't be patient because they are most greater in libido than women ... Because if our husband needs us and we dont come or obey them, then that man will find a way to get out his libido in his body, that is also one of getting sin to all men (taking other women) to fulfil the needs of thier body ... And we all know that Zinah (sexual intercourse to non (sic) of her wife or husband) is a great sin.

> *Aasiya* (quoting a Muslim feminist scholar, Ruqaiyyah Waris Maqsood): *In a truly Islamic marriage, neither partner should try to force the other one to do anything which is distasteful or unpleasant or painful to them.* (Aasiya continues) I am familiar with the hadith regarding a wife not coming to the husband's bed when he desires

intimacy. Now, what about the husband not coming to the wife's bed? To that, Sister Ruqaiyyah writes, *Since wives have the same rights in marriage as husbands, the same principle would apply if the husband refused the loving requests of his wife.* (Aasiya continues) The sister is correct! In other words, no double standard regarding sexual intimacy in marriage.

Hawwa: If he told you that he is willing to remarry again then accept his opinion coz a women obeys his husband will be rewarded in Paradise. As what i read from the Ahadeeth confirming of a wife who obeys his husband and it is narrated by Abu Hurairah (RA), that the Prophet Muhammad (SAW) said: 'If a women prays her five times Salaats, protects her chastity, and obeys his husband, she will enter paradise from which ever she wishes.' (Sahih Muslim) And there is also another hadith about a women who used to refused his husband on time he wants her wife to go on bed with him. ' And also the Prophet Muhammad (SAW) said: ' If a man ask his wife to go to bed with him, and she does not come to him, and he spend the night angry with her, the angels cursed her untill the morning.' (By Bukhari and Muslim). Remember sis that not only a women have a haqq (rights) to his husband, but also a husband have the rights for her wife. As what Allah (SWA) says:' Therefore the righteous women are devoutedly obedient (to Allah and their husbands), and guard in (the husband's) absence what Allah orders them to guard of(thier chstity and thier husband's property).' (An-Nisa V.4:34).

Aasiya: In all likelihood, men who were brought up thinking that they belong to the 'chosen gender' may get the idea that they can come home at any time and be verbally and/or physically abusive to their wives, repeatedly calling them out of their names, thereby making them (wives) look and feel like low-life trash. Yet, despite all of this, these men would still expect their wives to be sexually inclined to them, no matter what – just because 'that's the female thing to do.' If a wife doesn't have the freedom to be a firm, believing woman in her own home with her husband, then she's married to the wrong man, no matter how sexually lawful she may be to him.

Alma (to Nadja): Alhamdulillah, dearest sister. I am suggesting that no one has the RIGHT to aggress upon another, men or women. ... women should take responsibility for what happens to them. Studying the lives of the ummi muhminum (ra) I find that none of these women were sloven, or dependent totally on husband (whom was our Prophet sallallahu alaihi was salaam).

As the conversation cited above indicates, traditionalists regard sexuality as a sphere in which the wife should be available to the husband. They derive this understanding from the Qur'anic verse 2: 223 which reads: 'Your wives are your tilth unto you, so approach your tilth when and how you will'. Therefore, argues Nadja, wives must be always willing to have intercourse with their husbands, as it is their Islamic responsibility, provided that there are no circumstances prohibiting sex (e.g. menstruation; Qur'an 2: 222). This approach emphasizes most heavily the concept of wifely submission, the prime component of which is sexual submission (Mayer 1996). Shehada (2009) argues that in a contemporary Muslim context the equation of obedience on the part of the wife and maintenance on the part of the husband provide grounds for establishing marital relations. Sexual submission is linked to religious obedience, therefore a refusal to have intercourse with one's husband constitutes a sin.

Nadja also mentions verse 2:228 which says that women's rights over their husbands are similar to their husbands' rights over them. However, her understanding of this similarity is that wives are obliged to have intercourse at any time, whereas husbands only once every four months. Most traditionalists in the newsgroups develop arguments based on perceived natural differences in sexual libido between men and women, and on a more general level, in the psychological differences between genders that extend beyond biological difference as embraced by traditional Muslims (El-Sanabary 1994), and which 'cannot be ignored in the name of egalitarianism' (Nasr 1987). Due to what is seen as men's greater libido and more powerful sexuality (Dunne 1998) traditionalist participants claim that it is a wise marital strategy to make oneself sexually available to the husband, so that his sexual desires are channelled towards the wife, not other women (which prevents him from committing zina). The view that females have a naturally lower libido than men is propagated by traditionalist Islamic websites, for example www.islamonline.net, where a Q&A section dealing with sexual health reads: 'In many ancient and even modern cultures, the discrepancy between the male and female libido is so recognized that mothers hand down "secret" herbal formulas with instructions to their daughters on their wedding night … It is normal for females to have less sexual desire; therefore, this reality should not be viewed as dysfunctional or stemming from a lack of desire' (Burns 2001). Notably, this conceptualization contrasts with the projection of femininity as the source of *fitna* and sexual chaos that needs to be controlled socially while depicting masculinity as rational and capable of self-control (Dunne 1998).

Although Hawwa expresses her disagreement with Aasiya (an egalitarian) she does not use a confrontational tone and assumes that Aasiya is simply unaware of what participant Hawwa regards as the principles of Islamic marriage. In a similar spirit, Hawwa gives advice to another woman who is unhappy with her sexual life as her husband is impatient and hastens to intercourse without foreplay: 'sisters, I need help. My dh is very impatient in bed, he doesn't take time to prepare me before being intimate and I have pains in my lower body afterwards. I started pretending I am asleep when he comes to bed. Im afraid he will start looking for another wife, what should I do?'. Hawwa encourages the woman to talk to her husband, explain her problem, and ask him to be more patient in sexual intimacy; she also advises that if her husband wishes to marry a second wife due to this problem, she should not challenge his decision as that would be selfish. Sexual intimacy is regarded by Hawwa as a duty of the wife towards the husband, along with housework and raising children. However, she ends her posting on a slightly more egalitarian note, as she reminds the participant that husbands, just like wives, have duties in their marriage, which indicates that although women's duties are the focus of her contribution, she is aware that to some extent, marriage is a two-way process, and wives have certain Islamic rights. Finally, she sees the source of Aasiya's views in impatience and good-naturedly promises to pray for her to stay on the right path.

Even though most traditionalists stress the importance of satisfying a husband's sexual desires, some women who express traditional views on other topics focus on the importance of a wife's sexual needs, which indicates that there are varied perspectives on this issue in the traditionalist category. Afaf, who usually represents a firm conservative line on women's gender roles, shifts her position when it comes to women's sexual rights. She cites a hadith[10] in which Prophet Muhammad admonishes a man who prefers prayer and fasting over intimacy with his wife; the Prophet said that not only the Lord but also the man's soul and his wife and family have rights over him which must be fulfilled. She uses this example from Islamic history to indicate that a wife's sexual needs must not be ignored by her husband:

A sahabiyat divorced her husband because he could not satisfy her sexually. You can also read about Salman al Farsi, radhi Allaahu anhu [one of the Prophet Muhammad's companions], who advised a man who was married and neglected his wife. The principle of 'giving everyone their rights' came from that incident, ie, the body has its rights, the wife has her rights, and Allaah has His Rights. A man who has no interest or capability, and his wife is not being satisfied must make the effort, or else he is an oppressor.

This quote indicates that Afaf possesses knowledge of both the content of the Sunnah and the wider implications of the incident described in the hadith. She is aware that the hadith sets a standard for a couple's sexual relations, and she focuses on the prerogatives of the wife in this respect. Afaf's focus on women's rights and husband's obligations in the sphere of sexuality, suggests that women take a particular perspective depending on the subject of the matter and, possibly, their life experiences.

Aasiya, who is one of the strongest advocates of gender equality in her newsgroup, counters the traditionalists' argument on sexuality in Islam and states repeatedly that successful sexual relations are more likely to take place if male children are properly educated and taught respect for the female gender. She states that they need to be taught that in Islam, loving and respectful behaviour must be a prerequisite to sexual intercourse with a wife. In her view, happy sexual relations between spouses can only be based on equality and recognition of their respective rights to be active in both spiritual and worldly spheres; on the other hand, verbal and physical abuse by the husband indicates that this recognition failed to happen on his part and will prevent the wife from enjoying intimacy with him. The question of a wife's sexual availability to her husband pervades the comments made by Aasiya, as it is linked to problems of abuse and marital rape. The latter is sometimes justified as an Islamically permissible act, and verse 2: 223 is cited as confirmation of this (Touray 2006). Muslim women are also reported to have been battered on these grounds for refusing sex (Touray 2006). Aasiya links the argument in favour of gender hierarchy to the claim that a husband has an unlimited right to intercourse with his wife, both of which she regards as unIslamic. She receives support on this issue from participant Alma, who states that aggression and violence in sexual relations are forbidden in Islam.

Aasiya derides the idea of a husband's dominance over his wife, and the male gender being generally superior to the female gender, in contrast to the views of traditionalists, who believe that gender equality contravenes Islam (Kapiszewski 2006). Her belief in absolute gender equality in Islam is the reason why, in her view, the wife is not obliged to be sexually intimate with her husband upon demand. The fact that in her dialogues with traditionalists she situates those statements that emphasize the superiority of masculinity in inverted commas, indicates her ironic attitude and disconnectedness from these statements (Muecke 1980). Also, her use of swearing, an amplifying linguistic device, 'junk', in reference to the view that husbands have unlimited sexual rights, indicates her strong negative feelings towards this view (Kupferberg and Green 2005). Finally, on one occasion, participant Aasiya does not address Nadja, but refers to her as 'this sister'. This rhetorical move may be used to indicate her intellectual and psychological distance from her adversary's views (Crowley and Hawhee 1999).

Aasiya later raises issues about sexual education in the newsgroup, but some traditionalist women express their discomfort with discussing sexuality on a newsgroup forum, regarding it as a taboo subject, to be broached only within the family. This feeling has been also documented by researchers exploring the attitudes of Muslim immigrant families in the USA towards sexual education in schools (Orgocka 2004). A mother's embarrassment and limited knowledge of the subject may impede conducting such educative discussions at home, preventing young girls from obtaining knowledge as to their Islamic sexual rights and responsibilities (Orgocka 2004). On the other hand, Worth (2009) reports that Qur'an-based sexual counselling is extremely popular among Arab couples in the United Arab Emirates. He writes about Wedad Lootah, a counsellor in the family guidance section at the Dubai Courthouse, who is an author of a book on sexual education. In it, she addresses sensitive issues such as female orgasm and discusses particular problems experienced by her clients. As Mrs Lootah is still a pioneer, online discussions may be one of the few Islamically acceptable sources of knowledge on this subject for Muslim women. Aasiya argues that instead of being embarrassed, women should actively engage in conversations on sexuality in Islam, which to her is by no means vulgar, in contrast to what one of traditionalist women claimed. Aasiya's views are shared by those Muslims who produce and read educational and literary accounts of sex and sexuality online. Amir-Ebrahimi (2008b) writes about Iranian female bloggers who talk openly about their sexual experiences. These Internet expressions of sexuality are supported by such writers as Amina Wadud and Mohja Kahf who assert that the taboo surrounding women's sexuality must be broken down (Bunt 2009).[11]

Challenging Nadja's argument, especially the hadith about angels cursing a disobedient wife, Aasiya resorts to Islamic scholarly texts which advocate equality in marriage, also in sexual terms. She cites the book *Living Islam* where the author, Ruqaiyyah Waris Maqsood (1998), states that husbands refusing their wives sexual intimacy are also cursed by angels, thereby arguing for the mutuality of sexual obligations in marriage. The dialogue on sexuality, in which opposite points of view are firmly defined, continues with neither side willing to budge:

Nadha: Sister maybe you don't know the true rules of women to her husband. Yes you're right a women have his own rights too. But a man have his own rights to his wife so its the same? In Allah's sight we are all the same, man and women will go in Jannah but it is depend to thier good deeds and if how they work from it.

Aasiya: In other words, if he wants or demands to have sex with his wife 24-7 (Allah forbid!!!), the wife cannot refuse him. Really?? And all because 'he's the breadwinner'?? ... (If I told my two adult sons this junk, I can just see the looks on their faces, as if to say, 'Oops! Mama done lost it!' And they would have been right!)

Aasiya makes a move towards self-disclosure, relating her own sons' attitudes to show that she enacts what she believes in. She shows that she has managed to successfully raise and educate two sons who would rebut the idea of wives always being sexually available to them, and that she supports the point that a patriarchal treatment of women is a social construct, not a 'natural' state of affairs (Wadud 1999). This exchange attracted more contributors, who either supported one of them, or tried to reconcile their positions and create a middle ground. One of the negotiators, Raaida, suggested that the statement that angels curse a husband who refuses his wife sexual intercourse is an assumption, as Islamic sources do not evidence this, however, it is cited as being possible:

Raaida: I agree with sister Aasiya – but also I would like to say that yes while the angels will curse the woman who refuses her husband sex – we don't actually know if he will be punished for refusing her. What I mean is, there is no hadith or ayat that specifies that he will be punished as far as I know, but that doesn't mean its not possible – all is possible in the sight of Allah swt and Allah swt knows best. A husband has duties to his wife as she has duties to him. As far as

I am aware the reasoning behind the husband's needs being specified in the bedroom is a) because he is the leader of the family b) because it is a wife's duty to obey her husband but also c) men usually have higher sex drives then women. But that doesn't mean ours are not taken to be considered. Remember the Prophet pbuh said 'The best among you are those who are best to their wives and I am the best among you' and as we know he was known for his sexual strength in taking care of ALL his wives needs (sex I mean.). So in my opinion a husband should follow his best example insha'allah. And Allah swt knows best. Any mistakes are from me.

Raaida posits that a husband's rights are acknowledged and explained at greater length in Islam due to three important reasons. However, these rights do not impinge on a wife's rights – they are also considered and supported by the Sunnah and Ahadith, which is further emphasized by Barlas (2006). The sources report that Prophet Muhammad did not force himself on his wives, but still satisfied them in the sexual sense, thus expressing his love and respect for them. Through this, Barlas attempts to bring the two arguments together and achieve consensus, with regard to the sexual rights and responsibilities in Islam. It is also characteristic of this group that the women stress that what they say is their opinion, which, although based on their understanding of the sources, is personal. Holists do not attempt to provide absolute guidelines, but prefer to suggest certain points and encourage other women to make their own conclusions. They are also balanced and careful in their contributions as they point out potentially erroneous interpretations that they might unknowingly produce and disseminate. Finally, they attempt to introduce agreement into the newsgroups by stressing the importance of both spouses' desire to live in harmony.

Polygamy

Polygamy (Greek for 'multiple marriage') is a form of marriage to more than one spouse at the same time. In Islam, the only permissible kind of polygamy is polygyny – marriage of one man to up to four women. Polygyny is also the most common form of polygamy practiced across the world (Valsiner 1989). Polyandry, marriage of one woman to more than one man, is forbidden, therefore in this section I use the term polygamy to refer to the Islamic practice of polygynic marriage. While common in some Muslim contexts, such as the Arabian Peninsula states, in others, such as Western Turkey, it is virtually non-existent.[12] Al-Krenawi *et al.* (1997: 446) observe that in cultures practising polygamy its social construction is heterogenous, and depends on different 'social mores, values and customs', therefore it is important not to make transcultural generalizations when researching it.

The institution of polygamous marriage is not questioned as such by the majority of the participants, as it is a practice permissible in Islam, addressed in the Qur'anic verse 4:3, which says: 'And if you have reason to fear that you might not act equitably towards orphans, then marry from among women such as are lawful to you – two or three, or four: but if you have reason to fear that you might not be able to treat them with equal fairness, then (only) one – or those whom you rightfully possess'. However, it is not unanimously accepted as binding under all conditions, and women's positions on polygamy are very different. Aidah provides the historical context of the ruling on polygamy and concludes that it was politically beneficial for the early Islamic community:

Aidah: Some [polygamous] marriages [in early Islam] were with the view to help the women whose husbands had been killed while they were defending their faith. Others were with a view to cement relationships with devoted followers like Abu Bakr, may Allah be pleased with him. Yet others were to build bridges with various tribes who were otherwise at war with the Muslims. When the prophet became their relative through marriage, their hostilities calmed down, and much bloodshed was averted.

Sara: if a man is married once, he fancies or out of compassion marries an orphan eligible, lets assume; then he might start comparing the 2 wives, drawing more closely to the second to make her feel adjusted, neglecting the first, thinking that she would understand, etc ... all this sort of things may come from the cursed iblees [Satan].

Afrah: The fault of men is mainly due to lack of knowledge in their deen and not taking time to understand it, acknowledge it, learn it, apply it and then spread it. These are the basic fundamentals that one needs to adhere to in order to live a life upon the self inshaAllah. The fault of women is simple. Mainly because women are simple minded 99% most of the time and they run on emotional content and are very easily vulnerable, emotional, jealous, ignorant and many are arrogant to say the least.

While traditionalists agree that the reality of polygamy is sometimes far from the Qur'anic ideal of fairness, they see the source of injustice in either humans who are fallible, or *iblees* (Satan), mentioned by Sara, rather than in the institution of polygamy *per se*. Afrah blames all spouses if a polygamous marriage encounters problems, not the institution itself. However, she sees different faults in each gender, both of whom tend to fail in understanding the objectives of polygamy correctly. Whereas she sees the lack of commitment to Islamic education and following God's teachings as the main fault of men, she argues that women possess a range of emotional faults such as jealousy and anger, which impede the smooth running of a polygamous union. This construction of women as emotional and requiring control is characteristic of the traditionalist discourse which sees both genders as opposites (Dunne 1998).

Traditionalists argue that polygamy is sanctioned by God and that there are no limitations on the permissibility of the practice. In response to a participant who argued that polygamy should not be practised if it contravenes the law of the state, Afrah writes that God's laws are not restricted by political boundaries and apply to all believers; hence, Muslims are not bound by the secular legislation that bans polygamy.[13] Although Afrah admits that polygamous marriage may cause some difficulties, she sees them as a test of one's sincerity in applying Islamic values it to one's own life, thereby linking the practice of polygamous marriage with obedience to God in her argument:

> Allahu SubHanaHu wa Ta'la has prescribed that it is halal for men to marry up to 4. There are no stipulations except fairness in his dealings. ... No one is saying that it is easy in a polygamous marriage, and Allah SubHanHu wa Ta'la encourages fairness, but in order to become a better slave towards one's Creator, one must learn his/her religion, act upon it wholeheartedly and apply it in their lives, and then if able – spread it.

Traditionalists see embracing polygamy as an indicator of great piety and knowledge of Islam. In Sara's words, 'the most religious and knowledgeable sisters do not mind it but rather are open to the idea [of polygamous marriage]'. Some women, in order to give evidence of their love for Allah, look for co-wives in the newsgroups themselves, and as there are also appeals from single sisters wishing to become a second wife, it is likely that some Muslim women's Internet groups function as a platform facilitating polygamous marriages.

The issue of male libido, evident in discussions on sexuality, also arises in the debates on polygamy. In both sexual and polygamous contexts, it is linked to reflections on women's health and fertility. In the section on sexuality, one participant states that in case of a wife being unable to satisfy her husband's sexual desires he is entitled to marrying another. Similarly, other women argue that he is entitled to do the same thing in the case of a wife's barenness or poor health, which prevents her from being sexually active. Habiba insisted that her husband remarry when she was diagnosed with cancer as she believed that her husband had the right to enjoy parenthood and a sexual life. As she could not participate in either, but still needed her husband's assistance due to her illness, she perceived polygamy as a fair solution for all parties involved, although her husband refused to fulfil her wish:

Habiba: When I became sick I encouraged my husband to find a second wife but he said no and that he would take care of me ... I thought he had a right to be with somebody who could fulfil his needs. I thought then and still do, it would be better for him. He does not need to be nurse to me all the time and I would not want that either. He is entitled to a healthy wife who can cheer him up, be his mate, and help him when he needs it.

Traditionalists claim that the position of a second wife may be elevating and desirable; as there are more women than men, it is impossible for all men to remain in monogamous marriages if all women are to be married. It is pointed out that polygamous marriages assist divorcees and widows in the community. Similarly, Zeitzen (2008) lists reasons given by women for marrying as a second wife: financial support, a higher social status, love, and a preference for a relationship in which they had more time for themselves. On the other hand, in terms of the global demographics of polygamous marriage, Badawi (1995) points out that this type of marriage could not have been introduced by the Qur'an as a norm, simply due to the proportion of males and females at a global level, where the number of men and women are almost even. An assumption that polygamous marriage is recommended in Islam would require at least a gender ratio of 2:1. As such a ration does not exist, and as the Qur'anic norms are not based on 'impossible assumptions' polygamy should be an exception.

While in the USA, polygamy is associated with a lower socioeconomic status of immigrants from Asia and Africa (Bradley Hagerty 2008), traditionalist women in the newsgroups contradict this association by simultaneously stating that they are educated, thus representing a higher status, and that they wish to participate in a polygamous marriage, thereby fulfilling God's wishes. Nimaat makes such a statement, and adds that polygamy requires open-mindedness and generosity. She interprets other women's refusal to agree to their husband's union with her as jealousy, thus agreeing with participant Afrah that jealousy is one of the main faults of women:

> *Nimaat*: I am hearing sisters act like they hate polygamy or want to run from it. I must speak on this matter. I am an educated professional looking for a husband masha'Allahu ta'ala. And the brothers are few and far between. In my community the sisters don't allow the husband to get another wife (most of them). So that leaves me and other sisters out in the cold and struggling. It is sad how some sisters are so selfish to think that he is their property or that they have control over this.
>
> *Aliyah*: Alhumdullilllah I have very good news for you. There are literally thousands of good muslim men here [in Pakistan] that would love to marry you as a first and only wife. Now isn't that great! You too can have your own husband. These men here are having a hard time to even find ONE WIFE! NO SHORTAGE OF MEN! So how about lowering your monetary standards and marry one of these men who are over the age of 30 and still have never had a women at all!

Aliyah, an American who has been in a polygamous marriage in Pakistan, challenges Nimaat. The irony in her statement indicates that she is not an advocate of polygamy; however, she does not disclose any personal information that would explain her position. Aliyah's suggestion that Nimaat lower her 'monetary standard' is a concealed criticism of marrying for money and status. She turns the tables by pointing out that it is not only women who find it difficult to find a partner – men of a lower socioeconomic status simply may not be able to afford to get married; this phenomenon was also observed by Mallick and Ghani (2005).

In these encounters with different points of view, traditionalists are clearly uncomfortable with discussions of polygamy where negative views or experiences of it are included. They sometimes admonish women who either do not embrace polygamy or criticize the reality of it, for instance, by stating that in the face of injustices in the Muslim community, polygamy is not a matter that should be central to the discussions. Such criticisms of polygamy are seen as selfish:

> *Sadia*: It amazes me how we cry over polygamy/polygyny can gather the troops but will not open our mouths to blatant injustices perpetrated daily by us (women) and by men in our community to others daily. ... For us Muslim women to continue to dialogue in negative ways about the issue of polygamy/polygyny when we have so much to do in our communities is very selfish and self-centered.
>
> *Noor*: Sister, that is very unfair of you. We indeed DO speak up and try to help others in need to the best of our abilities. That does not preclude discussions on other subjects, especially one that is of great personal concern to us. Simply because you have chosen to be a second wife does not mean that you should try to squelch discussion of the impact polygamy has – which, in fact, is largely negative – on other Muslim sisters.

Noor challenges Sadia's statement, as she sees it as an attempt to change the course of the discussion to other problems (i.e. by ignoring participants' concerns about certain aspects of polygamy). She acknowledges that the Muslim community faces a range of problems, but disagrees with a claim that Muslim women are indifferent to others' difficulties. She does not let the conversation move on to a new subject and affirms that because polygamy is an issue that affects some women, it needs to be addressed within online discussions. Noor represents an egalitarian position and contradicts traditionalists' affirmation of it; she argues that although it is allowed, it is not obligatory.

As Souaiaia states (2008: 48), 'religion is used either to justify the practice [of polygamy] or to challenge its validity as a social innovation that has no place in the religious ethical discourse'. Thus, egalitarians firmly highlight the warning against injustice in marriage contained in the Qur'anic verse 4:3, and argue that when it is read in conjunction with verse 4: 129, which asserts 'You are never able to be fair and just as between women even if it is your ardent desire', the conclusion is that there is hardly ever fairness in polygamous marriages, so it is problematic whether it should be practised. This argument corresponds to the standpoint of Badawi (1995), who states that Islam has restricted and regulated the practice, not promoted it. In addition, egalitarians point out that it is possible for a wife to prevent her husband from acquiring a second wife by putting a stipulation in her marriage contract that the husband's second marriage automatically gives the first wife the right to obtain a divorce. Afsa provides information from an Islamic website to confirm this: 'As for the first wife. Well if she doesn't want a 2nd wife to deal with then she can have that written in her marraige contract and that is legal and allowed' (see islam-qa.com). As for women who do not have that stipulation, egalitarians argue that they have the right to be informed by their husbands who may have the intention to marry a second wife, because that is a sign of respect and kindness, qualities in marriage that are advocated by the Qur'an. Egalitarians are in favour of giving wives the option of getting a divorce if they are unwilling to be a co-wife.

Egalitarians point to what they see as a double standard in the traditionalist position, which is inherent in the suggestion that men are not required to look after a sick wife and instead are encouraged to find a younger, healthier, and more fertile one. Alternately, women are expected to operate as carers. Although there are voices among egalitarians that a wife is by all means entitled to divorce a sick husband and remarry, most women argue that standing by a sick or infertile spouse is a sign of love, which should not be compromised by including a stranger in the relationship for the sake of one's desires. In contrast to Habiba, who encouraged her husband to find a second wife as she developed a serious illness that prevented her from fulfilling her wifely duties, Hajar writes about her fears of her husband marrying another woman because of her infertility. She reports her relief on hearing her husband's decided response that polygamy contradicts his understanding of love. Therefore, she argues, he put the emphasis not on sexual or reproductive desires, but on affection for her, the beloved wife:

I have been married for 3 years and I cant get pregnant. As I have a child from previous marriage I always get worried about my husband's feelings. I asked him, what if I cant have a baby with you? He answered me: 'I cant love the child that I didnt have more than I love you, we will adopt a child, nothing will put us apart'. Because of this issue that we are discussing I asked him about the sexual aspect: Hipothetically, I said, If I couldnt satisfy you sexually and propose you to marry a second woman, would you do it? He said:' if you proposed me something like that I would divorce you right away because I would figure out that you were married to me because any other factor, like a house or position … when someone really loves someone, nobody cant share their intimacy.

Furthermore, egalitarians argue in line with Barlas (2006) that some men abuse the institution of polygamy. While it was introduced in order to encourage compassion for orphans and women in need, some may marry four wives to obtain a 'collection' of women to boost their self-esteem, like 'a guy (…) who bragged how he had 4 wives and had relations with all 4 every day and didnt need Viagra' (Maysoon). Participants also report that they know of men in their communities who do not support their multiple families financially, and 'sponge off their wives' thus going against the Qur'anic injunction that a husband is obliged to maintain his wife or wives (Dangor 2001). In addition, egalitarians point out that the position of a second wife, married to fulfill a husband's desires, either sexual or to have children, would be humiliating because she would represent, in Maysoon's words, 'a uterus for hire'.

Also, egalitarians do not agree with the traditionalists' claim that piety equals acceptance of polygamy on a personal level, as the dialogue below illustrates:

Sara: The most religious and knowledgeable sisters do not mind it but rather are open to the idea of polygamy.
Afsana: Sister, some women who are knowledgeable and religious are still not open to the idea of polygamy. While we acknowledge that it's a man's choice (not right), we also acknowledge that we don't have to choose to participate.

Egalitarians cite Badawi (1995) to argue that polygamy is not a sign of adherence to standards set by the Prophet Muhammad, as in that particular time of political and moral conflict this type of marriage was a solution that accommodated the needs of orphans and widows after the Battle of Uhud, in which many Muslim warriors were killed. The case of the Prophet is also viewed as an exception[14], necessitated by political conditions.

Egalitarians observe that women forced to be in a polygamous marriage can feel miserable and depressed, and this in no way could be a design of God. Moreover, some of the ex-co-wives write about feeling trapped, which negatively affected their faith. Shahnaz states: 'I dont believe that God who is alraheem and alrahman would want a believer to live in misery and hell because she feels trapped'. Research also reports a correlation between being involved in a polygamous marriage and high levels of depression and somatic disorders in women, especially first wives (Al-Krenawi *et al.* 1997). The transformation from an only wife to a first wife is described, based on women's accounts, as 'traumatic'. In Hassouneh-Phillips' (2001a, 2001b) research on experiences of polygamy by American Muslim women, all participants reported that they felt they were treated unequally in comparison to co-wives, a situation they saw as emotionally abusive. Al Krenawi *et al.* (1997) report a higher risk of depression, negative child health outcomes, low academic achievement and social adjustment in children born into a polygamous family, which is seen as a consequence of inadequate or dysfunctional exposure of the children to their father, and higher levels of family conflict. This is emphasized by Sayeda's narrative on her childhood as the daughter of a second wife:

> My mother was the 2nd of 3 wives. The kids suffer for this as much if not more than the women. Kids deserve to have their father at home spending time with them. Doing homework, going to the park whatever. As a kid you ask yourself what you did wrong that your father has no more time for you because he is too busy with THAT woman. Or how hurt you are when your father hasnt been around in a week but he took the other wife's kids (not his - from her previous relationship) on outings.. and wonder what you did wrong to deserve that.

She mentions a constant sense of deprivation regarding her father's lack of attention, as well as feelings of loneliness, low self-esteem, and a sense of injustice resulting from her father's polygamous union, thus she takes a strong anti-polygamy stance. She argues that no such union can be fair to any of the women, as it is human nature to favour one person over others. Her account also challenges the statement made by traditionalists who suggest that being one of the wives is better than not being a wife at all. This view is in harmony with El-Azhary Sonbol's ethnographic study of the lives of Jordanian women, where the husband's right to take a second wife is the 'most important source of fear for women' (2003: 131). Moreover, argues El Azhary Sonbol, the religious justifications for polygamy constitute some (albeit minuscule) consolation for women, who feel betrayed, heartbroken and disillusioned: ''There is no honor in your husband taking a second and third wife, no matter what the [religious] discourse says' (2003: 131). Clearly, women forced into polygamy experience it very differently from those who choose it willingly.

As the above example illustrates, egalitarians' and traditionalists' views on the applicability of polygamy are very different. Holists again try to reconcile these two opposite camps and find some middle ground:

Sabeera: You know polygamy is not for everyone, I don't think it is for me. Thank God it is not an obligation, lol but I don't speak against it at all. Some do better in a polygamous relationship. Someone wrote in about a woman who helps people learn Quran and this woman is physically disabled I think. If I am not mistaken this woman is a memeber of this group. This woman was married to a man that wanted to help her and to have her teach his children learn Quran. He already had a wife and the wife I think was more than happy to have her husband marry this second woman. It made their lives better to have this woman come into their lives. Like I said polygamy makes relationships better at times but it is not for everyone.

Mussah: I think a nice way to look at this polygamy issue is this. It is sunnah to live in Monogamy (as the Prophet did with Khadija) and it is also sunnah to live in Polygamy (as the Prophet did with his other wives.)

Both Sabeera and Mussah recognize that polygamy is not beneficial for every woman, and that Muslim women need to reflect on the issue before marriage. Then, they argue that polygamy is not detrimental for every woman, as some women may even feel better in such a relationship. They point out that everyone is an independent individual with different needs and qualities, and polygamy is definitely one of the marital options that requires careful consideration of one's personal preference. It is argued that regardless of the form of the marriage, trust and openness form the basis of its success; therefore, it is only fair that spouses discuss the issue of polygamy openly and with a full understanding of the Islamic teachings about it. Participants representing the 'middle ground' refer to the Sunnah, and observe that Prophet Muhammad practised both types of marriage, monogamous with Khadija, and polygamous with his other wives, thus sanctioning monogamy and polygamy as two different types of marriage which are recommended under different circumstances to different individuals.

This chapter has explored interactions between women representing different positions and indicated the commonalities and differences in their views on marriage, divorce, sexuality and polygamy, which, combined, constitute their understanding of the Muslim woman's personal sphere of life. Within the theme of marriage, I have analysed the sub-themes of power relations, expressed by the participants in discussions on marital obedience and hierarchies of gender; children's upbringing as a factor conditioning their later success in marriage; the marital contract as a strategy used by women to ensure that they have a say in the aspects of the relationship not regulated in detail by Islamic law; and finally, the choice of women's marriage partners. The theme of divorce has been explored on the basis of a female perspective on the right to be in a marriage that fulfils her needs. In my analysis of views on sexual intimacy, further links between views on gender equality and the right of women to sexual pleasure emerged, along with the sub-theme of sexual obligations in marriage. Within the theme of polygamy I explored the perceptions of libido and fertility alongside the concept of polygamy as an obligation, a right and a choice.

Discussions on private sphere issues help to expand the understanding of the views represented by each of the categories. Traditionalists emphasize the gender hierarchy where the husband is the head of the family and the provider who can expect obedience from both his wife/ wives and his offspring. On the other hand, traditionalist women are adamant that if the husband fails to fulfill his duty in studying Islam or if he attempts to stop them from correct practicing of Islam, they are likely to divorce him. As many of the traditionalists' marriages were arranged, they expect to be able to choose their children's marriage partners too. Their views both on sexuality and polygamy highlight that, in the face of perceived biological differences between men and women, husbands may expect their wives to be constantly sexually available, which is further enforced by the sense of obligation underscored by men acting as the providers. In cases where the wife is unable to have sex or children for health reasons, the husband is entitled to a second wife, as long as he can maintain both financially. Traditionalists see polygamy as an act that pleases God and brings reward in the afterlife.

Traditionalists' discussions revealed that in their argumentation they may significantly differ in their approach; while they argue for the same/similar outcome, they may do so for different reasons. Some traditionalists simply believe that their understanding of Islam and gender is the correct one, possibly because religious perspectives and gender roles are passed down in the family. They do not particularly wish to question the West as long as they are allowed to continue their lifestyle in peace. On the other hand, there are traditionalists who are likely to have, in some measure, adopted their understanding of gender relationships in reaction to the western claims of gender equality, often used in arguments by non-Muslims to produce 'evidence' that Islam is oppressive for women. These women's adoption of traditional understandings is more political and situated in the 'Islam vs. West' discourse. Amir-Ebrahimi (2008a) also observes this perspective in her study on Iranian religious bloggers.

Egalitarians' arguments are based on the premises that there is gender equality in Islam – they believe that marriage in Islam is a union of equals, and that such a concept should be instilled in children through positive role-modelling. In their view, it is integral to marital happiness that the union is made on the basis of piety and personal compatibility between spouses-to-be. They see divorce as a necessity in case where there is abuse and incompatibility in marriage. Sexuality is seen as a gift from God to be enjoyed by both spouses, with sex not being enforced on the wife, denied to her or her pleasure ignored. They challenge the traditionalists and argue that a 'greater' male libido is a social construct, used to control women through abuse of the concept of polygamy, which was sanctioned by the Qur'an and based on compassion, not lust. They see polygamy as a choice, not an obligation and point to some of the negative effects it has on women.

To some extent, holists' views combine the previous two positions, thus they create a middle ground while also acting as intermediaries, especially when discussions become very heated and there is a danger of a verbal fight. Holists argue that marriage is based on gender justice, where the rights and responsibilities of spouses are different but equally important. Similarly, they see sexuality as a domain of pleasure for both spouses, with the sexual rights of the husband outlined in more detail for practical reasons. In a pragmatic way, they see mutual rights and pleasure as a prerequisite for a happy union. Finally, they accept both monogamy and polygamy as equally lawful as they were both practiced by Prophet Muhammad.

The women's views on marriage, divorce, sexuality and polygamy are relatively polarized, possibly because they are related to very tangible issues. Although the marriagable age has risen in many Muslim communities, resulting in many unmarried women in and beyond their late 20s (Imtoual and Hussein 2009), absolute celibacy is not encouraged. Therefore it is anticipated that almost every woman will have entered into marriage at some point, which will require her to reflect on these four issues. This makes matters more personal and sensitive. These polarized views are mirrored to some extent by more general Muslim discourses, referred to by Engineer (2007: 74) as 'modernists' and 'orthodox Ulama'. As both egalitarians and traditionalists are becoming more entrenched in their views, the efforts of negotiators who claim that Muslim women have the right to choose their own life path become more visible. They point out that both the other groups may be right and that there is no need to become 'political', as individual context and personality dictate different views and choices. Through their attempts to bring the two opposite camps together, they emphasise the importance of sisterhood and unity as Muslim women.

The disagreements were expressed in a polite way, and by and large the women who challenged others did not do it on a personal level, but rather in terms of making an argument. Women did not assume that the other party displayed a lack of goodwill; instead, they expected that what in their view was an incorrect statement was caused by a lack of knowledge. This made most of the debates good-natured exchanges (although in a few cases some women felt afflicted by others' statements).

Women representing different categories read the Islamic sources differently and had different preferences in the choice of sources. As egalitarians and traditionalists represented opposite camps, differences between them were the most visible. Women representing the holists took on the role of offering a 'buffer zone', indicating points of consensus and shared interests. In the analysed discussions, egalitarians preferred to focus on the parts of the Qur'an that emphasise partnership and on modernist Muslim writers. On the other hand, traditionalists chose to use Ahadith, although they also referred to some Qur'anic verses. However, the ones used by traditionalists were the debate-provoking verses, read differently by different women. While egalitarians preferred to put these verses in the context of the entire Qur'an, a strategy promoted by Barlas (2006), who claims that this is the methodology of reading provided by the Qur'an itself, the traditionalists read Qur'anic verses literally and supported their interpretation with Ahadith, in the same vein as Abdul Rahman's (2007) observations.

Notes

1 See Sahih Al-Bukhari, Volume 4, *Book* 54, Number 460.
2 A hadith also invoked by traditionalists in support of gender hierarchy in marriage reads: "The Prophet said, if I were to order anyone to prostrate

himself before another, I would have ordered a woman to prostrate herself before her husband" (see Sunan Abu Dawud, *Book* 11, Number 2135). As in Islam prostration is conducted during prayer, traditionalists argue that this hadith indicates that the wife owes obedience first to God, and second, to her husband.

3 See Sahih Bukhari, Volume 9, *Book* 88, No. 119.

4 Qur'anic verse.

5 Lol is an expression used when communicating online or by text which stands for 'laughing out loud'.

6 American Muslim women are caught up in the conflict between two discourses: one of non-American Muslims who suspect that Americans cannot be 'genuinely Muslim' (see Chapter 7) and of mainstream American society, which argues that an American person cannot also be Muslim (Bullock 2005).

7 See Bukhari, Volume 6, *Book* 61, Number 582

8 See Malik's Muwatta, *Book* 28, Number 28.2.4.

9 See Sunan Abu Dawud, *Book* 12, Number 1273.

10 See Sahih al-Bukhari, *Book* 3, Volume 3, Number 189.

11 Here I am not referring to pornographic content, but texts that acknowledge the importance of human sexuality in Islam.

12 Tunisia is the only Muslim country that has explicitly outlawed polygamy (Douki and Nacef 2002).

13 It is reported that some Muslim men in the USA, especially immigrants from West Africa, secretly marry more than one wife (Bradley Hagerty 2009).

14 Prophet Muhammad, after his first wife Khadija's death, had nine wives simultaneously (see Sahih Al-Bukhari, Vol, 7, *Book* 62, Number 5).

4   Employment and mobility

In this chapter I focus on women's views on paid employment and dress code as two issues related to Muslim women's presence in the public sphere. They are explored alongside each other as women's negotiation of public sphere is inevitably related to the notion of modesty (Afsaruddin 1999). I investigate women's views on the permissibility of working in paid employment and the strategies they employ to negotiate gender expectations and their own preferences. I also explore women's notions of freedom of movement and how they interpret different rulings on women's mobility. In both sections I look at the interaction between participants and their willingness to accept other points of view on the discussed issues.

Employment

In the body of research on Muslim women and the public sphere, two streams are particularly relevant to Muslim women's online discussions related to paid employment. The first one focuses on the hijab as an item which enables Muslim women, both in Muslim-majority and Muslim-minority contexts, to transcend the boundary between the private and the public, join the labour market and maintain the reputation of being a 'decent woman' (Esposito and Burgat 2003). However, some authors have recently argued that a strong focus on the issue of veiling may silence those Muslim women who would prefer to focus on other significant issues that affect their lives (Ho and Dreher 2009). This criticism is well targeted in that literature on the hijab in the context of the public sphere, citizenship and community participation is very prolific whereas there is little literature providing an analysis of issues related to Muslim women and the labour market. There is a stream of research that examines the reasons for high levels of unemployment of Muslim (predominantly

Pakistani and Bangladeshi) women in the UK in comparison to women from other ethnic groups here (Brah 1993, 1994; Sly *et al.* 1999). Some recent studies focusing on Muslim women's paid employment have explored related issues such as the upward social mobility of working class Muslim women who increasingly attend university and engage in professional employment (Ahmad 2001; Mellor 2007). This is reflected by professions of those women in the newsgroups who state that they are in employment (IT specialists, civil servants, accountants, health workers). To counterbalance the dominance of the hijab debate, in this chapter I first focus on employment-related issues. I also address the question of whether Muslim women's mobility has a significant impact on the ability of women to undertake paid employment outside the home. Whereas a large proportion of participants did not consider any Islam-based restrictions as valid, those who represented the traditionalist category, especially those with Salafi sympathies, perceived the negotiation of mobility issues as integral to their crossing of the boundary between the private and the public.

Following a question on the permissibility of women working outside the home (and related issues, such as women's responsibility towards children and the costs of maintaining a professional career), participants submitted postings containing a variety of opinions. This was in line with Read's (2003) findings about the continuum between traditionalist and progressive attitudes to paid employment among Arab women in the USA. Balancing a career and a family is a prominent subject in online discussions. Participants mention several factors when considering the practical problems brought up by individual women who request Islamic advice. These factors include views on woman's work outside the home, the wellbeing of her family (emotional as well as financial), her spiritual and physical safety, and her individual talents and aspirations.

Egalitarians argue that relying exclusively on a husband's earnings has a negative impact on Muslim families, as it leads to anomalies in family relations, in particular inequalities in power. Aasiya criticizes the behaviour of some women who choose to give up their job upon marriage, which she interprets as lack of dignity and laziness. She stresses the importance of women's financial and intellectual independence from their husbands. Aasiya also points out the opposite problem – the 'hurt male pride' that emerges when a wife's income is higher than her husband's. She suggests that men who cannot come to terms with wives who are more successful in the professional field have problems with their own masculinity and should look for wives who are happy to be subservient:

> If a brother can't deal with his wife having more wealth or a better career than himself and is aware that he is not secure enough in his own manhood to cope. He should marry a sister who doesn't have these things or these needs.

Egalitarians accentuate Muslim women's right (or even obligation) to work outside the home and sometimes to even be paid for housework, a right that that women in the West have yet to win (Afshar 1998). The right to work outside the home is considered by egalitarians equally as valid as the right to receive an inheritance. Other justifications for women's employment and ability to generate an income are found in Islamic history. Khadija, Prophet Muhammad's first wife, was a powerful merchant (Ali 2003) and Sawda, Prophet Muhammad's second wife, was famed for her leather-craft which sold at high prices (Brooks 1995). Therefore, egalitarians argue, it is permissible for women to generate their own income and become financially independent:

> *Halah*: Well, it is not of my opinion of whether a sister should work or not. Islam gives her that right to work. So, in this regard my opinion or any other opinion, Allah has made the final decision on the matter. Many of the sahaba women had established occupations prior to the advent of Islam and maintained them afterwards. However, I will have to disagree that she need her husband's permission to work. It doesn't make sense for a sister to acquire someone else's permission to exercise this right … It as if saying the wife needs her husband's permission to receive her inheritance from her deceased parent(s), when the right has already has been established for it to be hers and not his.

In terms of negotiating paid work and housework, some egalitarians believe that their participation in cleaning, cooking, and breastfeeding their children is a 'courtesy' on their part. They argue that it is the husband's duty to ensure that the household is running smoothly, so for instance, he may have to (upon agreement with the wife) employ a cleaner, cook and wet-nurse. Saleema states that being taken out to dinner is "well within her Islamic rights". She also mentions that daycare is a perfectly permissible solution from the Islamic point of view, and refers back to the common custom of Arabic children being put into the care of Bedouins. The concept of being paid for housework and breastfeeding babies is popular among egalitarians, which harmonises with the findings of Afshar (1998) who reports that Iranian women's housework is waged and guaranteed by Iranian legislation. Egalitarians also cut short the attempts of other people to question their choices and, like Saleema who states that she "told them to mind their own business", assert their independence and preference for paid work:

> *Saleema*: I worked as an accountant for a Health Insurance company for a while, My dh did not care one way or the other whether or not my so-called Islamic duties around the house were fulfilled … His view cooking, cleaning, and bearing children are not the true essential elements of defining a good wife or a bad wife.

Egalitarians address the question of women's double work burden by arguing that women should not avoid employment on the grounds that they will need to work both outside and in the home. Those who do not refuse to do housework outright agree to perform half of the housework, with the husband performing the remaining half. They regard the belief in the priority of domestic roles for women as a non-Islam related, backward custom, characteristic of some Muslim communities, similarly to participants in Dale *et al.*'s (2002) research. Some egalitarians admit that this firm stand on the right to paid work is facilitated by the attitude of the husband. Those who dismiss household duties as activities they do not wish perform (and which they refer to, ironically, as 'so-called Islamic duties') mention that their husbands are 'relaxed', 'not bothered', or 'open minded', not opposing their wives from pursuing professional careers. This suggests that these women have selected like-minded husbands who support their wives' choices. However, one participant confessed that her dislike of cleaning led to her husband protesting and the marriage ending soon after. These accounts indicate that maintaining egalitarian standards requires either a husband who is wealthy and can afford paid help, or one who is helpful with regard to household duties.

Traditionalists disagree with egalitarians' belief that Muslim women's right to work is unquestionable. To them, women's right not to work outside the home is central (Franks 2001), and they see a range of problems arising from situations where women leave the home to work. First of all, they point out that work outside the home in most cases necessitates gender-mixing, which in their view is forbidden in Islam. Izma refers to Qur'anic verse 33:33, which advises women to stay in their homes. Other traditionalists write that some situations which might occur at work, for example, collaborative work with a male colleague, would lead to fitna (moral chaos). Second, they argue that a paid nurse will never be as committed as the child's mother in its upbringing, a point also raised by Badawi (1995). Finally, they state that women should not be deprived of seeing their children grow up, which is a great privilege, lost by most working women. Traditionalists maintain that female domesticity helps to maintain Islamic values, and child rearing by the mother ensures that these values are instilled in them:

> *Izma*: Sister, it is better if you look after the house and spend time with your children, as Allah (swt) made the woman to be the queen of the household and the man to provide for his family. I don't know if you have kids but it is a privilege to see them grow up. There are resplendent evidences in Islaam that require women to stay at home and not to go out except when necessary – for example in the Quran 'And stay in your houses, and do not display yourselves like that of the times of ignorance' (33:33). If you don't have kids, you may look for a job in a female-only environment (avoid gender-mixing!!!), but you need your hubby's permission to go out/work.

However, traditionalists are aware of the financial demands faced by Muslim families, especially immigrant families in the West, where kinship network support may be limited or non-existent. Therefore, many see women's paid work as permissible when the family is in financial difficulty. This concession has its limits; traditionalists, similarly to Badawi (1995: 18), argue that it is necessary for the wife to obtain her husband's permission to leave the house; in addition, they give preference to women-only workplaces,[1] as this environment protects women from temptation and sexual harassment. Finally, the domestic role has to remain a priority, with paid work being organized around it. Traditionalists, like egalitarians, recognize the fact that women in paid employment face a double burden of work, but they see the implications differently. Whereas egalitarians refuse to do any housework at all, or share it with their husbands, traditionalists suggest that, where possible, women should stay at home and abandon the idea of employment, thus limiting their burden of work to just the housework and child-care.

Jahida recognizes that social norms define the wife's position as being 'in the kitchen', regardless of whether she spends most of the day at work, whereas the husband is not expected to help out with domestic chores and is in a position to rest after his workday:

> *Jahida*: Yes, her [woman's] job in lfie is much more when compared to men, especially for working women. Some husbands help in household activities which is sunnah while some just dont even care; no matter how long she struggles in office; no matter even if both start from and return home together, most of the times, she has to go into the kitchen to prepare the food or arrange teh food or tidy up things while the husband relaxes ... What if instead she prays or cries out to Allah swt to help her lead life the way she wants, and what if Allah swt answered her? There would be no fights, no depression, no gulit, no iblees in between the couple.

This point is also highlighted by a participant in Roald's (2001) study, who argues that a Muslim woman working outside the home is as oppressed as a non-Muslim woman. In the second fragment of the quote Jahida suggests that a life a woman secretly wants is one where she is not burdened with the necessity of employment outside of the home. This freedom contributes to enhancing her marital life as she is more relaxed and domestically focused. However, traditionalists are aware that domestic work is not valued highly by society and instead seen as a 'non-productive' occupation for which no skill is required (Grandea and Kerr 1998). This problem of patronising attitudes towards stay-at-home mothers is addressed by Riffat. She reports that she was derided for not having a professional career:

> The main thing that I would like to share is that sometimes people feel when your at home that you are doing nothing and you are contributing nothing as they feel Money is everything:

Traditionalists, similarly to women in Afshar's (1998) study, go against mainstream perceptions and refuse to see housework as an unskilled, low-key job. Money, they argue, is not so important in comparison to the responsibility for raising the new ummah. They demand respect for it from other people, as they believe that motherhood and caring for the family home is a sacred and essential role. In contrast, women representing the holistic position believe that both lifestyles, as a professional and as a stay-at-home mother, are equally acceptable and Islamically valid (Afshar 1995). They give a number of reasons for this. First of all, they point to the different wives of the Prophet, some of who pursued careers, while others looked after the household. Second, they argue that as people endowed with different personalities, talents and dispositions, they need to follow their own individual calling:

> *Hijran*: Some sisters are better at maintaining the household and caring for the children, if they worked. While others are better at by staying at home. It doesn't make a sister any better or any less than the next if she chooses to do work and have a career. There used to be sisters who would make remarks about my havng a career, and small children. I used to tell them to mind their own business.

Hijran claims that those who accept their disposition will be effective and successful; in contrast, those who go against it will become depressed, stressed and take this tension out on people in their immediate surroundings – their family. Therefore, it is best if such a decision is left to the person in question, as only she knows exactly what her intuition suggests with regard to a career choice. Women should not be forced into either kind of employment, or derided for making a particular choice.

Finally, as the example of Ayeh shows, it is not impossible to enact both lifestyles at the same time (although again, such a workload raises the question of a double burden). She admits that although with difficulty, she manages to work in a responsible job as a web administrator for an online Islamic university, and because she works from home, she is also able to look after her baby. She states that she does not wish to give up working for the university, a job she performs primarily for a particular cause: spreading Islamic knowledge across the world. Ayeh's negotiation dovetails with Afsaruddin's (1999: 5) concept of 'carving out of public space by women for themselves, sometimes paradoxically by not even leaving the home, through which space they are able to derive benefits for themselves and impose their presence on society at large'. The benefits for Ayeh include having an independent source of income and a level of self-satisfaction; it is also clear that she is able to exert an important influence on her employer, whom she supports with her skills and effort (she has had to adjust to USA working hours, as she lives in Pakistan).

Ayeh: I am website administrator and provide all teachnical support to an online university. I have to work on extreme hours ... In the begning it was really great. But after I got married and Saad (my son) was born it became rather difficult for me to manage the job, home and baby. I do work for the university as its cause is really good. I live in a Muslim country and I never knew how difficult it is to raise Muslim children in a non-muslim society. Now I know what problems they are facing. They don't have good teachers and don't have good islamic school on which parents can trust. I think IIU is a timely effort for these Muslims. Even though it is really difficult for me to manage so many things, but I love the cause of this university.

Holists argue that women can pick and chose from different lifestyles, for instance, like Mina, who has switched between their roles as an employee and a stay-at-home mother, and Asalah, who has switched between the roles of a stay-at-home wife and an employee. Both report having acted on their inner needs, and both are satisfied with their choices, especially because they are aware that if they wish, they can switch back again with the full support of their husbands:

Mina: I left my career for a minute. I just got tired of the fast pace lifestyle and wanted to spend time with my kids. So here I am 1 year later and enjoying. At times, I miss my paycheck, but you know when my last child is in school, I can pick my life back up and keep on achieving the things that are sought by myself. *Asalah*: I would like to share my thoughts & U wont believe it that am writing from my office now. yessss am a working woman, got a break in July last year then resumed my work last week only. I really enjoyed my days when I was not working& asked for a beark from my husband cz wantd to give time to myself & I enjoyed cz there was no restriction i could get up for Fajr & pray & read Quran and all & i even used to go for Tajweed & tafseer classes as well and MASHALLAH have learnt a lot of Surahs & am striving hard to keep up with my Tajweed class now that I am working.

Both Mina and Asalah express satisfaction about the ability to make choices based on their Islamic rights; it is important that this freedom is financially supported by their husbands. They give different reasons for their decisions to temporarily suspend paid employment: Mina wanted to spend more time with her children while Asalah wanted time for herself, which she spent studying Islam and praying. They both mentioned that the intense life that resulted from working outside the home prevented them from pursuing their priorities, but did not entirely write off paid work. Asalah seems to be happy to be back in the office, having intensified her spiritual endeavours, and Mina points out that she can concentrate on herself and pursue her interests and goals. The role of the husband is important in both accounts, as his financial support is a prerequisite to the wife's choices, affecting the financial situation of the family. Presumably, single women and mothers and women from families with a low socioeconomic status would not have had this opportunity to withdraw from the labour market.

Mobility

It is argued that restrictions placed historically in Muslim societies on women's mobility and activities are disappearing (Weiss 1994). However, the question of Muslim women's right to free movement should not be approached with a view that seclusion of women was a preferred social order in the past, and with time it has been rejected as an anachronism. Today, religious justifications of women's mobility restrictions are created either by traditional scholars (Kapiszewski 2006) and women themselves, and I examine this discourse in the newsgroup context (where most women participating in these discussions are American), by considering traditions related to respect and honour (Weissl 1994), or by looking at the legislation from a number of states which in enforced by different types of 'morality police squads' (Moghissi 1999: Ahmad 2005). I look at ways in which women justify their decisions and understandings of Islamic sources in regard to mobility, including leaving the house, going on longer journeys and driving, by examining a newsgroup discussion stimulated by a member's question regarding Islamic proof with regard to women travelling without a *mahram*, unmarriageable relative or husband who escorts her:

> *Juwariyah*: I strongly disagree with this [ban on women travelling alone]. I must travel alone at times and it can be for some period of time. My husband cannot accompany me everywhere. I conduct myself in such a way that there is no doubt that I am to be left alone. People naturally keep their distance with me as my body language says I am wishing to be undisturbed when I am traveling. I am fully

covered (with the exception of niqab since I don't wear it) and I don't engage in unnecessary conversation with strangers as a general rule. At 43 years of age, I hardly think it is necessary to have a chaperone!

Sanya: Even if we conduct ourselves properly in hijaab and manners, this does not then make it permissible for us to travel about without mahram as Allah and His Messenger (saws) have been clear on this, masha'Allah. The 'ulemaa have also addressed the effects travelling without mahram have on our eemaan (faith) and insha'Allah if I find these articles I will post them. Islam is not to suit our desires or opinions. A hadith that says that a woman is not travel except with a mahram is here: transmitted by al-Bukhaaree – No.1862 and Muslim – No.1339 and its authenticity is agreed upon (by both al-Bukhaaree and Muslim).

Juwariyah: I will continue to disagree because the Qu'ran does not say I must restrict my actions. Also I have grown weary of hearing Surat al-Ahzaab (Ayat 36) used to justify shutting a person off from making a decision that is contrary to your own. It has not been proven to me that it is necessary for me to shut myself in the house just because I'm not able to travel with my husband when I conduct business in the outside world. Wives of the Prophet were not kept as prisoners. Sister, I feel as if you are so pontificating that I resist *everything* you say because of this. You need to look into your heart to see if your intentions are as pure as you claim they are. I do not subscribe to your way of thinking and am not likely to on many issues. I don't want to cause fitnah and after this I will not respond to your messages because I know I feel compelled to argue with you when I should not. It is better that I withdraw politely and engage myself in other activity and discussion which is better for my heart and my iman.

The discussion over the matter of women's mobility without the company of a mahram includes two conflicting points of view which are represented by Juwariyah, an egalitarian, and Sanya, a traditionalist. Juwariyah's argument is based on practicality; as her husband cannot accompany her when she is travelling in connection with work. She states that her own moral conduct: wearing the hijab, avoiding socializing with strangers and not acting flirtatiously, gives her the legitimacy to conduct her affairs outside the home without the need for accompaniment. In her opinion, her mature age also ensures that she acts responsibly and in a satisfactory way in terms of Islamic principles on women's conduct. When challenged by Sanya, Juwariyah defends her position by displaying Islamic knowledge; she identifies one of Sanya's statements as a Qu'ranic verse, and claims that this verse is abused by those who, like Sanya, believe that their interpretation of the Qur'an represents the meaning intended by God and try to impose it on others. In addition, she makes a reference to early Islamic history and uses the example of the Prophet's wives as enjoying freedom of movement. This is in the same vein as Badawi's (1999) view that women in the times of the Prophet enjoyed full participation in the public sphere. Finally, she dismisses Sanya's argument as Islamically legitimate and refuses to continue the conversation, as, in her opinion, their understandings of Islam are too distant from each other to overlap and further conversation would lead to fitna, chaos and disagreement. Juwariyah also questions Sanya's intentions in this exchange; she suggests that Sanya's challenges may not be due merely to her Islamic convictions.

Sanya's position is that Juwariyah should not continue her employment if her husband is not able to accompany her while travelling to work. In her opinion, adhering to a proper Islamic dress code and the Islamic rules of behaviour are not sufficient to justify women's free movement. She invokes the authority of God, Prophet Muhammad and scholars (ulema) to support her view; she also refers to a concrete hadith addressing the issue of women's mobility. Based on scholars' opinions, she regards travelling alone as negatively impacting women's faith and conduct, and she interprets Juwariyah's position as ignoring the word of God to suit her own needs.

However, a controversial topic and the ensuing firm positions attract the attention of holists who address the disagreement in a more cheerful way and try to find some middle ground. In order to do that, they come up with a number of reasons why limitations on women's mobility may have been introduced. Others, like Muminah, reformulate the rather bold previous statements, so that the debate continues on a number of additional levels, not only with regard to rights and restrictions. Muminah's narrative indicates that her lifestyle is similar to Juwariyah's (she works and commutes on her own), but she stresses her preference to travel with her husband as a more enjoyable activity than travelling alone, not seeing it as a hindrance or restriction. She regrets that her husband is a stay-at-home type and does not like to go out with her, but admits that commuting in his company would be unrealistic as they work in different locations:

Muminah: well I would love to be able to convince my husband to accompany me everywhere, but usually it's the opposite. ... he never wants to come with me when I take my son to play at someone's house or visit friends etc. or my family and of course, it would be logistically impossible for him to accompany me to work as I commute to New York & he works in New Jersey ... that would pose a real hardship for both of us – so I think it's certainly preferable to travel with my husband, it's not at all realistic for me.

Other women, including Maryam and Aqsa, emphasize the safety factor. Maryam takes a historical perspective and considers the requirement for women to travel with a mahram in a context of military conflicts of early Islam, where women without protection were in danger of harassment or an attack. In her opinion, reinforced by her reading and information gleaned from lectures, while this requirement was valid in the past, currently it has lost its urgency, as safety is ensured by designated services, for example the police force:

Maryam: There are different rulings concerning this matter, depending on which scholars one follows. From everything I have read, and heard in lectures on the subject, the original prohibition was based on women not being safe when traveling long ago. This is not necessarily the case now. It was meant as a means of protection for women who were unable to travel safetly, not a means of oppression.

Aqsa refers to the authority of the President of the Fiqh Council of North America, an 18-member group of Islamic scholars that decides judicial issues for North American Muslims. Her consultation with him indicated that women's safety when travelling is a priority, and when it is ensured, it is permissible for women to travel alone. She also refers to unspecified Ahadith that are supposed to confirm this:

Aqsa: I had consulted with a scholar, the prez of the fiqh council of north america, on exactly this matter and according to him it depended on where I was traveling, with the reason being safety. There are apparently other ahadith on the subject too which are usually not quoted (and i certainly dont remember them) which would indicate the issue is of safety only, and if that is ok, then women can travel.

As the ban on women driving in Saudi Arabia is justified by the traditionalist religious discourse (Mayer 1995), women in the newsgroups also debate its legitimacy. The participants who live in large non-Muslim majority countries, such as the USA and Canada, are particularly interested in the Islamic perspectives on women driving, and in some women's opinion, the long distances they may have to cover when travelling necessitate the use of a car. One newsgroup member posted a question on the permissibility of women driving as she was confused that in some Muslim-majority countries women are allowed to drive and in others they are not. In response, another participant posted an extensive article by Sheikh Abd al-Azeez ibn Baaz,[2] who served as Grand Mufti of Saudi Arabia between 1993 and 1999, which explains why, in his opinion, women should not drive cars. This includes the reasoning that there is the danger of mixing with men while driving as well as a belief in women's limited intellectual capacity which may endanger their and others' safety (Abdul Rahman 2007). Khalida, a niqabi, takes a practical attitude in her engagement with ibn Baaz's text,[3] which she responds to in smaller segments:

People have spoken a great deal in the al-Jazeerah newspaper about the issue of women driving cars. It is well known that it leads to evil consequences which are well known to those who promote it, such as being alone with a non-mahram,

Khalida: How does my driving put me alone with a non-mahram? He explains later, because a car breaking down. What if I am walking on a road without much traffic and I twist my ankle or worse yet break it. Half an hour later, a muslim man drives by. He can stop and help, you know. This is not "free mixing" and it is not haram to walk, yet walking may lead to haram mixing (he could stop and exceed the bounds of what is permissible in talking or touching).

unveiling,

Khalida: Perhaps the sheikh does not realize that many women in america drive fully veiled, with eyes showing only. And they can see just fine. Before I was Muslim, my hair used to get in the way more than my niqab does now. The niqab itself doesn't prevent good driving.

and committing haraam actions because of which these things were forbidden. Islam forbids the things that lead to haraam and regards them as being haraam too.

Khalida: Yes, if you're driving to a bar to socialize, because it is leading to something haram, it's haram to drive to a bar. It is halal to go to the store to meet a need, so it's halal to use halal transportation to get there.

Women driving is one of the means that lead to that, and this is something obvious,

Khalida: Subhan'Allah, this may be an excuse made by women, that they remove their niqab because they "feel better" when they do, when driving in various countries. But that is just an excuse. It is completely possible to remain veiled and drive safely!!!!!!!!!!!!!!!!!!!!! He must not be aware of this. How would he know about driving with a face veil (since he doesn't wear a face veil, and also, Sheikh ibn Baaz, may Allah be pleased with him, was blind, so he also didn't drive), except what the women around him inform him? A car is just a tool. It can be used for good or evil. A man can suicide bomb in a car. Are cars haram for all men in all circumstances, because sometimes some men use it for something haram? No. If a man is driving to a bar with the intention to drink alcohol, is the actual drive halal? No

In response to ibn Baaz's argument, that driving may lead to immoral acts, Khalida emphasizes the importance of the intentions with which a car is used. In her view, driving in itself carries no moral value, what does is the purpose for which it is used. The potential to commit immoral acts may not provide the grounds to ban its use, especially that it is not the grounds on which to ban men's driving. Khalida uses the example of driving to a bar in order to drink alcohol as equally haram for men and women, yet, she observes, men are not banned from driving.

A second argument she engages with, reads that women's driving is immoral because it leads to unveiling; however, she argues that even a face veil does not impede driving, as long as the eyes are uncovered. It is indeed possible, as shown by the example of American niqabi drivers. In a further part of the article, ibn Baaz claims that driving threatens women's personal safety, with which a larger group of participants disagree. Khalida explains that in the American context, where due to the hijab or niqab Muslim women are easily discerned by non-Muslims, they are more likely to experience harassment on public transport, especially if they do not have a male relative or husband to accompany them:

As salaamu alaikum, I feel it is safer for a woman to be in a car as well. Like I said before, there are many muslim women who don't have a man to allow them to do anything. Me and my household are an example. Muslim women are the ones that stand out all over the world and even riding on a donkey is not enough protection.

It is clear that although traditionalist women would prefer to adhere to traditional rulings (that women should not mix with males outside the home or drive cars), necessity forces them to negotiate theory and practice. Muskan writes: 'In regards to driving, I believe that its a neccesity, most of us don't live close to things to be able to walk comfortably or safely to our destination. While I would love to let my husband do all the driving, I still must play "MOM's Taxi" for school, drs appt, grocery store etc.'

This chapter highlights the interconnectedness of the themes of paid employment, and women's mobility, also identified by Secor (2002), who concluded that a woman's choice of veiling or not may expand or limit, her mobility and access to employment, depending on the context and its dominant discourses. This has been confirmed by women's narratives in this study which have also addressed the relationships between women who may or may not represent a similar hermeneutical position. Göle (1997: 61) writes: 'In Muslim contexts of modernity, women's corporal visibility and citizenship rights constitute the political stakes around which the public sphere is defined'. Participants' voices in this study indicate that women have taken on the task of defining the boundaries of the public sphere themselves, by reflecting on and negotiating the meanings of their choices for them, their families, and their communities. Although women's heightened visibility in the public sphere is the priority on the egalitarian agenda, it may not be a sufficient marker of empowerment; the variety of positions suggests that it is women's capacity to choose their own life path and others' acceptance of these choices that ensures empowerment.

The discussions make it clear that for Muslim women in a non-Muslim majority context, there is no easy win regarding their behaviour in the public sphere. Regardless of their position, they have to display a degree of non-conformity to deal with those challenges that are inherent in their interactions with some of their Muslim sisters, families and communities, as well with as the non-Muslim community. Newsgroups are a context where their choices are negotiated and chiselled through interaction with a range of positions.

Notes

1   Muslim women creatively fill niches in the market with their women-only services, for example women-only taxi companies, popular in the Middle East, are springing up in the UK (Firth, 2008).
2   Available in full at *www.islam-qa.com/en/ref/5849/doc (accessed on 9 June 2009).*
3   Italicized for clarity.

5 Sisterhood

Introduction

As the two previous chapters focused on the priorities of egalitarians and traditionalists, the views of the holists have been presented mainly as attempts to find the middle ground between those two positions. However, women representing holistic views also have their own agenda, which is different from egalitarians' and traditionalists' priorities. A more detailed analysis of the holistic viewpoint allows us to go beyond the limiting binary egalitarian/progressive-traditionalist/conservative viewpoint, which to a large extent defines contemporary studies of Islamic understandings (Zaman 2008). This chapter explores the ways in which holists attempt to strengthen the bonds between all women, which is their first concern. I also look at their attempts to create an atmosphere of friendship and support in the news groups.

An online Islamic sisterhood in the global context has not been the focus of many academic studies to date.[1] Zaman's (2008) observation that most studies of Muslims adopt an ethnographic approach, instead of that based on interpretations, also applies to most works that focus on Muslim women's online activities Brouwer 2004a, 2006; Bhimji 2005; Amir-Ebrahimi 2008a, 2008b). This chapter is therefore an important contribution to emerging research on the sisterhood of Muslim women, forged on a transnational scale, and from where they try to look beyond their own positionality. The significance of this perspective lies in the fact that many Muslims today do not see Islam as an 'inherited aspect of their ethnic identity', but fashion their religious identity based on a hermeneutic approach, which is defined by interpretations of Islamic sources (Zaman 2008: 465–6).

The concept of sisterhood is at the root of most of the newsgroups which include a reference to sisterhood on their public web-pages.

Newsgroup creators explain that sisterhood is the female part of the ummah, and do not exclude any women on the basis of their allegiance to a particular school of Islam, or because of social class, age or race. In most cases they are also inclusive of non-Muslim women, who are welcome to join the groups as long as they are respectful towards Islam. Their focus on sisterhood is also reflected by the newsgroups' names, which often contain the word 'sister' or 'sisters'. These characteristics suggest that the newsgroups were created with the intention to bring women representing different hermeneutic positions, ethnicities, and social groups together, which sits well with holists' views.

Contested sisterhood

In one of the newsgroups, an atmosphere of anxiety emerged following an incident where a member was removed from the group due to her aggressive behaviour. There was a wistful discussion among the women about the threats of the Internet, where one can be faced with having to deal with undesirable individuals. Some women commented that even private newsgroups, described by the academic literature as religious women's Internet havens (Griffin 2004), turn out to be places where one cannot trust people. This is where Sareenah intervenes, referring back to the ideals which led to the creation of newsgroups. She highlights the reasons why the groups were created, and what the advantages of participation are. Finally, she pleads with other women not to lose their sense of trust and to continue posting to the newsgroups:

> I think this group is a great thing to have because some sisters dont have any other way to 'connect' with fellow sisters in Islam and I myself have been cheered up on a bad day or a 'lonely' kind of day by ALL the email waiting for me in my box knowing that many sisters were with me in 'spirit' and it feels good to know that and have those reminders (…) insh'allah everything shall be good in the future integrity of this group. Jazakumallah Khair … **please continue to fill my mail box with all those wonderful reminders of sisterhood in Islam** @};–

Sareenah highlights two aspects of sisterhood enabled by the newsgroups – spiritual and emotional connection – also identified by Bastani (2001) as particularly important to those women who do not have the opportunity to interact with other Muslim women in a face-to-face context; and support, a specific type of connection, which seems to be very effective in the newsgroups considering that discussions on Islamic laws are frequently commenced by participants posting a question or a problem for others to comment on. While some address an Islamic perspective from which an issue may be approached, emotional support is provided equally often. Sareenah's reference to many sisters being with her in spirit indicates that connection with other women may in fact constitute support, as it alleviates the sense of loneliness.

Holists often bring a positive tone to the discussions, but sometimes they bring more clarity to situations when discussions begin to bear signs of a conflict. One such exchange developed following a participant's account of discrimination which she experienced as a Muslim living in the USA. A number of participants discuss other kinds of discrimination Muslim women were subjected to (racial, gender, classist, ageist), and they concentrated on their own experiences, instead of supporting other women. Shahida commented in response:

> Not once in all these 'annoyed' discussions have I heard Islamic responses to the hurt (which is the product of anger) or anger (which is the product of hurt) for these posts. Pre destination is an Article of Faith of Islam ... each of us are born where we are because it was the place Allah intended us to be born. What we do with our lives and how we practice Islam in our lives and how we treat each other is what Allah looks at ... not all these labels being bandied in thse emails. I hear prides voice from the black and white .... I hear railings from the discriminated against ... I hear so much ... but I don't hear the spirt of truth of Ramadan.

Shahida's narrative indicates that she refuses to participate in discussions which are held by what she sees as self-centred individuals. She highlights the need to use Islamic knowledge to solve practical problems; this, in her opinion, is the best way to approach challenges, as Islam is a complete way of life and provides answers to all questions, as long as one is willing to look for answers (Wadud, 2005). Her denunciation of 'labels', which function as a basis for discrimination, suggests that she embraces the vision of ummah as one where diversity is celebrated. Shahida also addresses predestination as one of the doctrines of Islam,[2] and emphasizes the need to accept God's will, which determines one's current position on Earth; therefore, focusing on the challenges one faces due to that position means ignoring its positive aspects and constitutes ingratitude. In the further part of her posting, Shahida evokes the example of Prophet Job, who accepted God's will with humility, and sets him up as a role model for the Muslim community who concentrate too much on their involvement in the *dunya* (this world), and forget to put any effort into developing a spiritual connection with their Creator. However, she does not advocate separation from people, but engaging with them in a compassionate way:

> Most of all that I have read serves Satan ... that sisters be divided ... filled with hurt, offended, angry. Where is the empathy, compassion? There is much division among Muslims for many reasons ... was not this said to happen? and it has ... Each of us can chose to be part of the division or not. What ever happened to forgiveness and understanding ... ???

There are two processes which Shahida identifies in today's Muslim community: division and unification. Division is strongly condemned by the Qur'an in verse 3: 103: 'And hold fast, all together, by the Rope which Allah (stretches out for you), and be not divided among your selves.' Such division can be understood in a number of ways: institutionally, as the emergence of new sects of Islam, and socially, as the alienation and discrimination of certain groups within a community. Shahida sees the latter as leading to the former, as she associates division with feelings of hurt, offense, and anger which damage the social and institutional ideals of the ummah and sisterhood. On the other hand, Shahida understands forgiveness, empathy, and compassion as values that should be intrinsic to interaction among Muslims. In a similar vein, Hassan (2004) links the concept of ummah to these values and explains that the term 'ummah' comes from the root '*umm*' (mother), which indicates that ummah should be like a mother to the believers – compassionate, caring and forgiving.

> *Shahida*: Today I see sisters in this group rant at each other ... busily pounding their computer keyboard to answer a letter with a sharp response ... which is worse? that we kill each others bodies.. or we kill each other's souls and our own by the tone and content of what we say to each other and the slights we give and the resentments we harbor ... does not Allah forgive when we are not deserving? What is your response to forgiving the undeserving?

That particular discussion does not meet the ummah/sisterhood standards in Shahida's eyes. She does not appreciate the way other members use the newsgroups to take part in open conflict with other women. A comparison she makes has a strong message – the conflict which is developing is 'killing souls' – both of those targeting and the targets, which is worse than death.

Some participants in that discussion expressed a wish to emigrate from the USA to a Muslim-majority country due to the Islamophobia they had experienced, hoping that they would feel more accepted in a country representing their own religion. There were a number of responses suggesting that Muslim-majority contexts are not free from prejudice, and Faeeza wrote:

> I once made the comment to some very wise brothers and sisters very close to us ,that I wanted to leave and live in a muslim country. Well brother gave us some very good advice. He told us that we should stay right here. Islam is the fastest growing religion in the USA. He said that we should put roots here grow in our communities and keep close and spread dawah. Grow and flourish … Sisters this is why we should be close to each other. Visit if possible,if not, email. Unite our sisterhood,do dawah and love each other, for Allah said so … I know how it feels to be mistreated and abused by non muslims. That is why its important for us to be kind to each other. To love to be in the company of a sis.

Sustaining and developing the sisterhood network is Faeeza's priority; she sees both face-to-face and online contact as legitimate ways of interaction. This contact has to be grounded in positive attitudes within the ummah; as well as dawah to support the growth of Islam. She represents the view that emigrating to a Muslim-majority country constitutes escapism, which does not solve the problem of challenging prejudices; instead, she advocates remaining in the USA and changing the context, in terms of promoting both Islam and tolerance. Although she does not construct the ummah concept in opposition to the non-Muslim population in the USA, she argues that Islamophobia, which she also experienced, simply necessitates the unification of Muslims. In other words, it makes Muslims responsible for supporting each other in these difficult times and makes the mistreatment of Muslims by Muslims even more unacceptable.

Sisterhood across hermeneutic divisions within Islam

This focus on Muslim unity is shared by those women who comment on another situation reported by Lama, who reports she had been met with a frosty welcome from a niqabi in a mosque who did not return her greeting. Lama suspects it was due to the fact that she was wearing 'only' a hijab on that day instead of a niqab, which she wears frequently otherwise.

> *Lama*: (…) I mentioned it to my intended and he told me that Salafi don't consider you muslim if you are not Salafi. Therefore they do not salaam you. Is this true?!?!
>
> *Rumanah*: I am shocked to hear that you were treated that way … it really upsets me to hear that Muslims are behaving so arrogantly. You would think if someone knew at least a little about Islam then they would know better than taking part in sects. I never say I am anything other than Muslim because that is what the Prophet (peace be upon him) was recorded to have said and nothing else if I am not mistaken. We as Muslims need to understand this. *I couldn't care less about what each sect does though I don't see harm in finding out about different ways of life* [emphasis added]. If we are Muslim then we should say and others should treat us as if we are Muslim whether they have their doubts or not because Allah is the only one who can say who truely believes and who doesn't. Not just some niqabi in the masjid, it is not her call
>
> *Lama*: Jazakallahu Khairn for the beautiful words Alhamdulilah they mean a lot to me. Incha'allah I will remember them when next I am hesitant to speak to the next sister out of fear of rejection. You are right, Masha''allah, I should not take leave of my duty as muslim (and it IS our duty to greet them and then reply with equal or better) just because they may not reciprocate as Allah (SWT) sees all that is in our hearts.

This exchange indicates that representing holist views may be imbued with difficulties and internal contradictions, as the belief in the unity of all Muslims is not shared by everyone. It also demonstrates that qualities related to holists, especially embracing the diversity of Muslims, are closely linked to the concept of ummah/sisterhood. This is reflected in the belief that one does not have the right to make judgements on other Muslims' faith and choices, as the fact that they claim they *are* Muslims should be sufficient; their truthfulness cannot be truly established by anyone else than God, who is all-knowing. Therefore, Muslims do not have the right to alienate other Muslims on the basis of their perceived piety, and attempts to do so are illegitimate. This response removes Lama's doubts as to her future course of action (she was wondering whether she should still greet Muslim women of the Salafi school). Lama took on board Rumanah's comment, which, although made in the context of the niqabi's behaviour, suggested that if Lama chose not to greet another sister, this would be based on her personal judgement as to whether the sister would greet her back or not, and making a judgement of this kind might be entirely unjustified. Therefore, it is better to approach everybody with an open heart, holding on to the knowledge that what ultimately counts is pleasing God with one's actions, not the potential rejection of another person.

Rumanah, similarly to Shahida, takes a firm stand whereby competition between schools of thought within Islam is discouraged. She refers to an unspecified hadith which reports that Prophet Muhammad never advocated the creation of sects and insisted that 'Muslim' is the most important religious identity. This position is also supported by Shireen, who similarly stresses that being 'just Muslim' is absolutely sufficient:

As long as we are sincerely following Qur'anic guidance and the Sunnah of the Prophet (Allah's Peace be upon him) to the best of our abilities, it is irrelevant what madhab, manhaj, or school of thought we belong to. Above all else, we are MUSLIM, MUSLIM, MUSLIM!!

The existence of hermeneutic differences within Islam is accepted by Shahida, Rumanah and Shireen; however, what they emphasize is that these differences should not be a reason to prioritize or impose any particular interpretations of Islam on others (as long as these interpretations genuinely help to develop understanding of Islamic sources and do not abuse them). This is a belief in Islam which is not a monolithic religion, and which has the capacity to contribute to the wellbeing of the Muslim community across the world. The holists' view is encapsulated by Ramadan (in Cesari 2004: 152), who said: 'The true Muslim comes to understand himself in the rigorousness of his conversation with God, and in the Muslim community by initiating dialogue with those who think differently from him'.

In a discussion following the report of the mosque incident, Rumanah points out that she is willing to engage in dialogue by saying: 'I don't see harm in finding out about other ways of life', while at the same time asserting that she does value her own life path choice. This openness to others' views while retaining one's own independence and the right to make choices is also reflected in Shireen's attempt to establish a code of practice that would apply to online discussions between Muslim women:

Engaging in 'I'm right and you're wrong' and 'my scholar is better than your scholar' scenarios serve no useful purpose. This only breeds impatience, intolerance for other views than our own, bitterness, and unwarranted attacks on sisters' iman and/or character. By showing off how 'knowledgeable' you are, you're only making yourself look ignorant, immature, and insecure. Nothing is proven or accomplished by trying to 'prove' other sisters are 'dumb in the Deen'.

Academic literature differentiates between relational conflict, which is about personal style, values, political and religious preferences and knowledge; and task conflict, which is about interpretation, procedures and policies (Amason and Schweiger 1997; Jehn 1997). There is a view that while task conflict is more related to the task than the people who perform it, it is less detrimental to the final outcome than relational conflict, which leads to negative judgement of one's personality and beliefs (De Dreu and Weingart 2003). Shireen's efforts to prevent conflict on a relational level are a good example of how best to facilitate online discussion, as she suggests that personal attacks do not yield any positive outcomes. She discourages actions and statements that attempt to introduce a hierarchy of knowledge into the groups by commenting that such moves reflect one's ignorance.

Sisterhood across divisions based on the path to Islam and race[3]

A heated discussion on judgements developed after a newsgroup member made a disparaging comment about converts who, she thought, never wholeheartedly convert to Islam and instead remain faithful to their old non-Islamic views (in this case, she referred to another participant's supportive comments on feminism). Group members unanimously disagreed with this comment, instead constructing a common discourse that highlights the need for openness and lack of judgement in interactions among Muslims. In the course of the discussion, participants referred to a number of kinds of discrimination for which there should be no tolerance in the ummah. These include unequal treatment due to the school of Islam one follows and covering, as already mentioned, but is also due to being a convert, which introduces a racial dimension, and highlights one's socioeconomic level. Racial discrimination among Muslims has been discussed by Karim (2008), who explored the factors that contribute to the emergence and enforcement of divisions within the American Muslim community. Karim reported that in predominantly Asian Muslim contexts suspicion towards converts (either white or African-American) resulted in converts overcoming racial divisions socially and creating 'convert communities' (2008: 142). Jaiyanah does not believe in enforcing racial divisions:

> This attitude and these types of statements are EXACTLY what pushes people AWAY from Islam. What right do you as an individual have to judge another person's sincerity in accepting Islam? These types of statements are exactly what causes me to walk into a masjid where sisters refuse to return my Salaam because well, since I'm 'American' I can 'really' be Muslim in their eyes.

She challenges racialization of Islam by pointedly attending sermons and prayers in mosques which are dominated by Asian Muslims. Through her presence, she attempts to mark the mosque space as a Muslim space, regardless of the ethnicity of the believer. Her narrative indicates that she has been socially rejected a number of times, but she continues to regard her presence in these mosques as a message of Muslim unity. Her opening sentence indicates that Muslim unity and the inclusion of all races in integral to the growth of Islam, which is expanding globally due to the rising number of conversions (Lee 2002; Aidi 2005).

Women who have converted mention 'otherizing' by Muslims as one of the most significant difficulties in post-conversion life. Discrimination by non-Muslims, who may discriminate against them because they see converts as 'race-traitors' (Franks 2000) is accepted more resignedly, as something expected; however, ostracism at the hands of their new brothers and sisters in faith is a cause of disillusionment. Many women convert in anticipation of joining a sisterhood that transcends racial boundaries, and they find this may be a myth; this was also observed by Karim (2008). Khuzanah narrates her experience of post-conversion interaction with her friends and relatives and indicates the twofold alienation and racialization of Islam by a non-Muslim and a Muslim she was close to:

> When I first reverted to Islam I encountered two incidents: First was when I told my mum I had become Muslim she said 'yeah but your not Asian?' And the second time, a former Pakistani 'Muslim' friend said to me 'Why, you're white?' ... We need to teach the world, and better still, our fellow Muslims that Islam came for the benefit of all mankind and not just Arabs/Asians'

Khuzanah then describes Islam as a religion that was bestowed on entire humanity, but for historical reasons, Arabs and Asians were the first to benefit from it. Arabs, as the first people to embrace Islam, went on to gain followers through winning military campaigns in Asia. This resulted in the contemporary association of Islam with particular ethnic groups in the common consciousness, as literature evidences, in both traditionally Muslim (Zeleza 2005) and non-Muslim majority contexts (Górak-Sosnowska 2007). Khuzanah further addresses previous postings sent by the 'convert-criticism' thread initiator, and identifies her own appeals for the acceptance of difference. Thus, she exemplifies this by selecting social groups with whom her sympathies lie: men, mothers, and Pakistanis and Indians. Khuzanah challenges the discrepancy between the other woman's request for openness and tolerance for groups she regards as discriminated against, and her own stereotyping of converts:

> On one hand, you are sending out emails warning sisters about passing judgement on men & the mothers & Pakistani/Indian culture & on the other, you, yourself are sitting in judgement of EVERY revert in the world. What right do you have to do that?

In spite of some disappointments, women in the newsgroups by and large continue to believe that a sisterhood which transcends racial boundaries was made tangible by Prophet Muhammad in his the last sermon.[4] He emphasized the common ancestors of all humanity and the equality of all races, perhaps envisioning misconceptions that might arise from the fact that Islam was originally given to Arab people or referring to racial discrimination likely to have existed in early Islamic Arabia (see Lewis 1985).

> *Sameena*: There is NO better group of people in Islam. Allah t'ala sees us ALL on the same level, no group is superior to another. One

only has to look to the Prophet's sallahu alehi wa salem last sermon to see that where he says: 'All mankind is from Adam and Eve, an Arab has no superiority over a non-Arab nor a non-Arab has any superiority over an Arab; also a white has no superiority over a black nor a black has any superiority over white except by piety and good action'.

Sameena complements this excerpt with Qur'anic verses 30:22: 'Among God's signs are the creation of the heavens and of the earth and the diversity of your languages and of your colours. In this indeed are signs for those who know' and 49:13: 'O people! We have created you from a male and a female and we have made you into nations and tribes so that you may come to know one another', which, she argues, constructs the politics of racial equality in Islam. She writes: 'a distance between where we are now and the Qur'anic ideal may exist, but it is our responsibility as Muslims to shorten it as much as possible, and this should be our mission'.

Sisterhood across socioeconomic differences

Giving to the poor is prescribed in verse 2: 83 of the Qur'an which reads: 'Worship none save Allah (only), and be good to parents and to kindred and to orphans and the needy, and speak kindly to mankind; and establish worship and pay the poor-due'. In discussions on Islamic charity, zakat, one of the five pillars of Islam is often considered, although strictly speaking, zakat is not charity, rather, it is an Islamic right of the poor members of the society to have a share in the resources controlled by the wealthy (Richardson 2004; Kochuyt 2009). It is an obligation of the wealthy to the needy. In return, the person who shares his or her wealth is promised a great reward in the afterlife. The collection, management and redistribution of zakat is conducted by formal institutions, such as the Central Zakat Council with local branches in Pakistan (Richardson 2004). In contrast to zakat, sadaqah is a 'voluntary, heartfelt gift offered on one's own accord' (Kochuyt 2009: 111).[5]

There is a strong emphasis in the argument of holists that an Islamic sisterhood should include Muslim women of all social class backgrounds, and become a vehicle, not only for interaction between the women, but provide charitable help for those in financial hardship. The charity function of Islamic social institutions has been explored by a number of authors, for instance, Clark (2004) investigated how, in the

Middle East, Islamic social welfare services are inextricably bound to the middle classes and defined by horizontal connections. Clark emphasizes the informal character of Islamic social institutions, in which trust, solidarity, and teamwork develop. Over the last two decades, a rise in the number of NGO Islamic social institutions in the Middle East has been identified both on national and international levels[6] Benthal and Bellion-Jourdan 2003; Roy 2004); these NGOs have taken on the role of social security providers in countries where 'governments have been disinvesting in the social field' (Kochuyt 2009: 13).

In the context of western non-Muslim majority countries, some Muslim thinkers call on Muslims to concentrate upon civic awareness based on the social message of Islam, which has to be rooted in a personal sense of responsibility (Ramadan 2004). This sense of responsibility determines one's actions, such as spending, coexisting with one's neighbours, voting and serving one's fellows. Online discussions indicate that this recommended sense of responsibility is strongly felt by the participants, who recognize the need to help the less affluent in their immediate communities as well as fellow believers living further afield. Arshia describes her and her friends' Eid annual gift action in terms of aiding a Muslim woman of limited means:

> Like this Eid, there is this one sister whose husband can't alway buy her the nice fancy overgarments. So we decided instead getting each other an Eid Gift, we will put our money together and arrange a gift certificate at a local ladies store for her to get two or three of them for herself. You know that is what sisterhood, helping each other instead of snubbing each other.

Arshia considers such help, on a relatively small scale, as an expression of sisterhood. The independent decision to replace the tradition of giving each other Eid gifts with the collection of gift vouchers for another sister suggests solidarity, generosity, and sensitivity to the needs of others. Although clear about their wish to share their resources with others, participants also discuss the danger of emerging unequal relations between 'sisters who give and sisters who take'.

In line with the Qur'anic prescription about the need to perform charitable acts inconspicuously (Kochuyt 2009), so as not to humiliate the recipients, Arshia reports that she and her friends are discreet about their gifts. It is also worth noting that they do not give away old, unwanted items of clothing which might be humiliating for the receiver;

they instead present vouchers which give receivers the opportunity to go and pick new outfits themselves. Raya sums up what the ideal of the Muslims' interaction should be: 'we are all muslim and it does not matter what you have or don't have or where you from, we are cool people who love Allah and His Messenger which is our lifeblood for sisterhood'. In her statement there is a connection between overcoming differences, the love of God and sisterhood. The online discussions suggest that participants recognize the need of giving to the needy, both when celebrating, and in everyday life. Ithar states that small good deeds contribute to a huge and important outcome which is improving the ummah; she further argues that worldly luxuries are rewards from God which have to be shared with others and not taken for granted:

> You know if Allah, blessed you with something, do good with it. If you are blessed with a new Lexus or a nice little minivan, and you see that sister you know (or you don't know) standing at the bus stop with her kids, pick them up and take them where they need to go.

Ithar points out that helping others has to be extended towards one's immediate circle of friends and acquaintances, as achieving a global sisterhood must be initiated by expanding one's interest to other, unknown women in the vicinity. This focus on localized interactions with people corresponds with Ramadan's (2004) appeal for taking responsibility on a personal and community level, which should be a foundation for activity on a larger scale. This kind of activity, comprising work and donating to national and international charity organisations, such as Sista2Sista, Inc.,[7] is regarded significant in expanding the sisterhood. Sista2Sista helps those women who have to financially maintain their families, for example, due to a husband's accident, deportation or death. Appeals list individual cases, with specified numbers of family members including the number of elderly and children. Atiqa encouraged others to support this charity by adding sayings of the Prophet in relation to the charity, including 'The most loved actions to Allah are: Happiness you give to a Muslim, or Sadness you take way, or Debt you help him with, or Hunger you put away, supporting my brother in one of his needs is better for me than staying in this mosque for a month'.

Islamic Relief USA and Islamic Aid and Helping the Needy UK, are considered equally important. Ruqayah comments on Al-Qaradawi's article, in which he argues that personal change has to precede attending demonstrations, giving to charity and talking to the media when injustice against Muslims is happening (Al-Qaradawi's article was written after Israel's attack on Gaza in December 2008): 'The article overall is good but I disagree with Yusuf Al-Qaradawi where he states we should not do anything until we change ourselves first. Change can take time for some people and that shouldn't be our excuse in not helping our fellow Muslims in need'. In the period following the occupation of Gaza, participants forwarded a large number of appeals for financial help from international Muslim charities.

In these discussions about charitable acts, participants do not make many references to Islamic sources; these are saved for debates where points of view are advocated and argued. The need to sincerely engage in sharing with others is not questioned; women refer only in general terms to sisterhood and pleasing God by giving to charity.

Sisterhood or feminism?

In the already mentioned discussion initiated by a group member who expressed her doubts about converts' sincerity, a parallel thread developed. As she commented on a convert's sympathy for feminism, participants began debating the merits of feminism in the Islamic context. As discussed in Chapter 1, feminism's relationship with Muslim women has been an uneasy one. Western (secular) feminists have often defined Islam as a paradigmatic case of patriarchy (Varisco 2005). Feminist writers living in Muslim countries, like Mernissi (1985), argue that Islam has facilitated and supported patriarchal systems. In response, El Guindi (1999a) stated that Mernissi's argument was reductionist as it focused exclusively on just two factors impacting women's position: gender and sexuality, ignoring others, such as class, ethnicity and age. This dialogue is parallel to exchanges between second- and third-wave feminism (Henry 2004).

Muslim women's opinions of feminist developments in the West vary, as they focus on different aspects and periods of the non-Muslim feminist struggle. A regularity, also observed by Badran (2001b), that characterizes these discussions is that women who reject feminism, in line with Abdelatif and Ottaway's (2003) participants, refuse to see a variety of positions within the category 'feminism'. They tend to address the radical strands of feminism which reject marriage and family as intrinsically patriarchal structures. On the other hand, women who see an overlap between their and secular feminists' interests, point out that they agree with *some* postulates of feminism because they were previously made by Islam 14 centuries ago. So, while one group of women disregards or ignores feminism[8] on the grounds that it cannot give them anything worthy of attention that Islam has not given them already, another group tends to make connections with non-Muslim feminists; this is on the grounds that both Islam and feminism support women's rights. In this section I investigate whether this binary is maintained by the newsgroup members.

An unnamed thread initiator explains why, in her view, support for feminism must be incompatible with full, genuine support for Islam. This is carried out in an earlier discussion where she challenges another participant: 'How can you say your muslim and yet at the same time support something (feminism) that is against the teachings of Islam. Islam teaches the union of the two genders not women are better than men or vice versa'. After her comment on converts, and posting a link to an article which states that feminism is incompatible with Islam, she never comes back to argue her point further, although it is likely that she reads the replies. In spite of no response from her, participants still address her (they do it directly, by writing 'you') and make their positions clear:

Lubna: The definition of feminism is: http://dictionary.reference.com/ search?q=feminism 1. Belief in the social, political, and economic equality of the sexes. 2. The movement organized around this belief. This is absolutely in keeping with Islam and Islamic values. The writer below wants to take some far-out examples and say that that is what all feminists believe. Shouldn't you as a Muslim know better than that?? Isn't Islam even as we speak being maligned by those who warp its teachings and go off on tangents? You should thank God for the activist feminists who have come before you so that you can vote, own property, have an independent bank account, own your own person, play sports in school, choose your major and on and on.

Samia: i am a muslimah revert and i would just like to say that i have never been behind feminism. all its done is ruined the family values as the mother is too busy doing her so called career. don't get me wrong have a career i had a beauty salon and i still study so when my children are able to cope with less help i will continue. my hubby and i have a 50/50 relationship. if i am feeling unwell then my hubby will take over the housework and the children.

Lubna: Salam I am pro feminist, but not the lesbian hate the man version of it. Feminism supports women in choosing the life they want to lead, including defining what is important to them. Do not tell me what I believe and I will let you live your free life, provided to you on the backs of the feminists who came before you. *Ameerah* (responding to the thread initiator): Can you PLEASE get what is called a DICTIONARY and define the word before using it wrongly. Feminism is just the idea of equality between women and men, like the definition sis J***** got from dictionary.com. Now, if you are against that, then you might as well change your last name to your husband's (or future husband's) ... Why do you think in Islam, the woman doesn't change her last name [when she gets married]? I feel that is such a smart thing alhamdulilah! And yes, that is part of feminism! So is that wrong? Of course not. *Shamila*: you go girl!!! lol;) I agree ... 'islamic feminism' ... Omid Safi in his essay said that if that strikes anyone as an oxymoron then it is unapologetically suggested that it is THEIR version of islam that needsrethinking ... not his.;)

Lubna: feminism is not a western concept btw,[9] islam is very much a feminist religion whats wrong with those of us saying were feminists meaning we don't believe men have the right to treat us like their personal slaves ... to me thats called feminism ... and to top it, its Islamic feminism.

[signed] Loubna
who must be quite evil since I go in the mens way at the masjid cuz i cant be bothered walking allll the clear way around the masjid to go into the stupid womens side ... dats femnism, cuz men need to lower their gaze and respect us women!!!

In this discussion, Samia is the only one to express an anti-feminist sentiment, which is based on the popular traditionalist belief in the detrimental effect of feminism on the family, especially children, who are separated from a mother who works. Samia equates feminism with paid work; however, she elaborates on her own family life, which could easily be described as feminist: she owns a business and is studying, therefore she is dedicated to exploring her personal potential and increasing her financial status; in addition, she describes her relationship with her husband as 50/50, which is thus an equal partnership. This indicates that her dislike of feminism is only nominal or partial, as she accepts and implements in her life a number of feminist principles. Williams and Wittig (1997: 901), in their exploration of women's resistance to the feminist label, suggest that many fear the 'evaluative connotations that they carry and those of others'. The fact that she mentions that she is a convert may indicate that she wants to escape the stereotype of a western woman who is inevitably tainted with the feminist sympathies.

The argument in defence of feminism as defined by Lubna has two varieties: Islamic and practical. Some participants emphasised the compatibility between Islam and feminism in that both (according to different women), struggle for gender equality or justice. Ameerah uses a very specific example: she states that both feminists and Muslim women are unlikely to give up their maiden name,[10] thereby retaining their own identity after marriage. Taking a husband's name after marriage is seen both by many Muslim women and western feminists as humiliation and an indication that the wife belongs to the husband (Afshar 1993; Twenge 1997). Ameerah specifies other concepts which are, in her opinion, common goals of both Islam and feminism: 'Equality of the sexes, same pay for same work, job security and maternity leave, education of women are not antiIslamic concepts'.

Lubna refers to a Muslim scholar, Omid Safi (2003), who, in her opinion, aptly summarizes criticisms that claim Islam and feminism are compatible, in the introduction to his edited volume. This suggests Lubna's interest in, and knowledge of, current scholarship in the area of Muslim women's studies. She makes a claim that feminism is not a western concept, but, she suggests, an Islamic one, a claim which is based on the Islamic recognition of woman's full personal status. There is a parallel between this recognition (which transfers women from the category of a dependant, or, as some women would argue, a slave, to that of an independent human being), and Lubna's statement that feminism prevents women from letting men treat them as 'personal slaves'. Thus, Islam and feminism are qualified as parallel, liberating forces. Finally, Lubna makes a disclosure which reveals that she actively implements her philosophy: she challenges the spatial gender division of the mosque and does not pray in the women's, part, but in the main, male section.

A second argument in favour of feminism is underpinned by a practical approach to life, where Islamic arguments are not employed. Feminism, these participants argue, is the only way forward in making individual or family life better.

Ameerah: There is nothing wrong with a woman having a life! Some women have a need to get a job, because of the low household income. Or some of them just want to do something. At some time, all the children are gone. Either they are all at school, or they all graduated, or they all have families of their own. Either way, the women should have the choice to do something on her own.

Shamila: To me, both the woman and the man are responsible for their children in every way. You never know who may be gone the next day. What if the wife is? The man will at least need to know how to change a diaper, or make cereal. And there's nothing wrong with that.

Women look at the specific reasons why feminism may facilitate day-to-day activities; Shamila points out that women should have the choice to do something that is not related to children or domestic work, especially as children grow up and leave the parental household, causing women without any independent activities feeling potentially abandoned or isolated. Here, the defence of women's non-domestic work is often constructed as a defence of feminism in the face of traditionalists' criticisms that women's careers 'ruin the family values' (which was earlier suggested by Samia). An opposite situation, where a husband may be required to undertake domestic, traditionally female roles, is addressed by Shamila. In case of a wife's absence, sickness or death her husband must know how to look after their children, and this can be only acquired by his equal participation in the household duties.

On a different note, Raniya links support for feminism to the acquisition of civil rights by women:

What those 'awful' feminists suffered for YOUR right to vote ... The women were innocent and defenseless. And by the end of the night, they were barely alive. Forty prison guards wielding clubs and their warden's blessing went on a rampage against the 33 women wrongly convicted of 'obstructing sidewalk traffic' ... So, refresh my memory. Some women won't vote this year because – why, exactly? We have carpool duties. We have to get to work. Our vote doesn't matter. It's raining.

Raniya emphasizes sufragettes' perseverance and dedication to the women's cause by providing a graphic description of their sufferings. She indicates that all women (regardless of their religion) owe suffragettes respect and gratitude for securing this political right. Raniya states that contemporary women's gratitude should not be limited to words of support for feminism, but extended to the act of voting which is neglected by many women in modern democracies. Raniya's response indicates that many participants may appreciate not only their economic and social rights, but also their political rights within society, which harmonizes with the reformist Muslim scholars' view that political participation is a legitimate, or even required, activity for Muslims in non-majority contexts (Ramadan 2004).

Sisterhood is constructed by holists as an all-embracing concept that transcends various divisions along the lines of: hermeneutic Islamic position, school of thought, path to Islam, socioeconomic status, but most importantly, race/ethnicity and the related concept of culture. As holists operate within online contexts also populated by egalitarians and traditionalists, they often find themselves in the 'firing line', but by employing a strategy of inclusivity they stand out as a relatively strong fraction. It does not mean that they accept everybody; while they put much effort into seeking agreement in the online debates, they combat attempts to introduce any dividing lines. This is particularly clear in their challenges of other members who make disparaging remarks about other Muslim women, or indeed even non-Muslim women, as illustrated by the heated debate on feminists. An opening line of one such challenge reads: 'Excuse me sis, haven't you learned in Islam NOT to judge anyone?!' This message is characterized by politeness, expressed by the phrase 'excuse me' and the use of the term 'sis' (short for sister); forcefulness, stated by writing 'not' in upper case and an exclamation mark, as well as by a reference to Islam – in Islam, one has no right to judge others and their intention as this is exclusively God's prerogative. This is paradigmatic of holists' attempts to teach their fellow members what they see as a code of practice of interaction with other Muslims.

Holists argue that it is a duty of every Muslim to support unity of the ummah, which they see as an Islamic requirement, laid out both by the Qur'an and Prophet Muhammad, so separatist remarks are perceived by holists as a breach of an Islamic principle and combated with dedication. A second point holists make about Muslim unity is that it is particularly significant in the context of confrontation with the non-Muslim world. While they are far from preaching the need of confrontation in the manner of political and religious extremists, they are pragmatic, recognising that a rift between Muslims and non-Muslims exists, and Muslims in the West, still stereotyped and othered by the mainstream, non-Muslim population, are likely to experience abuse and discrimination. In this situation, holists see division within the Muslim community as especially harmful: 'If we ever hope to strengthen the Muslim sisterhood, we've got to stop being so judgemental of others'.

In the consideration of the holist perspective on sisterhood, the triad: egalitarian-traditionalist-holist, clear in previous chapters, is not valid. Participants shift their attention from the gender factor and examine relationships existing within the female Muslim population; they 'regroup' debate about the responsibility they have been assigned in order to help prevent injustice in relation to race and class. Those (relatively few) who do not support this effort are seen as the opposition. Both egalitarians and traditionalists may be in the latter group as they sometimes criticise each other heavily, if on different grounds. However, opponents are included in the debate and vigorously argued with.

Notes

1 Bastani's (2001) study is an exception.
2 There have been disputes among Muslim theologians whether predestination takes precedence over free will. For a further discussion, see Souaiaia (2007).
3 Based on this division, women define themselves as 'converts'/'reverts'/'new Muslims', or 'born Muslims'.
4 Available in English at www.islamicity.com/mosque/lastserm.htm (accessed on 10 June 2009).
5 Although sometimes the Qur'an uses the terms zakat and sadaqah interchangeably, sadaqah is a wider term; as Şentürk writes, 'every zakat is sadaqah, but not every sadaqah is zakat' (2008: 5).
6 The Middle East has a much longer history of charity being delivered by Islamic organisations, in particular, in association with the activities of the Muslim Brotherhood, which developed its charity networks in the 1930s (Talhami, 2001: 313).
7 http://sista2sista.org/default.aspx (accessed on 22 June 2009).
8 There are also vocal non-Muslim anti-feminist women (see http://awomanagainstfeminism.blogspot.com/) as well as those who reject feminism, saying that it has achieved its goals and is not necessary anymore – they are defined as post-feminists (Aronson 2003).
9 btw stands for 'by the way'.

10 Retaining the maiden name after marriage is a religious requirement
  (Abdul-Rahman 2007: 292), and may additionally be a social (Camara 2007)
  and a legal (El Guindi 1999b) requirement in some Muslim-majority states.
  This, as Afshar points out, is still a patrilineal practice as women continue
  to rely on male surnames (1993).

Conclusion

This book has explored the new Islamic expressions and dialogues that are taking place across state boundaries and other divisions based on race, ethnicity, class, age and, perhaps most importantly, across different understandings of Islam. The Internet, as a medium, may reinforce the regulatory Islamic discourses produced by scholars, thus strengthening their authority, but it simultaneously opens up new discursive spaces within which Muslim women from varied backgrounds study and interpret Islamic sources together; in the course of their discussions they engage with others' positions and acknowledge each other's right to have a personal understanding of Islam.

Moreover, this book informs the debate on Muslim women's contemporary expressions, as it has discovered that Muslim women's global reinterpretation of Islam at a grassroots level has already begun. Women studying Islam's scriptural sources are not a new phenomenon, as Ahmed (2006) identified women's interpretations of the Quran during the time it was still recited. However, it is safe to assume that these interpretations were always more or less contextualized – produced by women who knew each other, and experienced similar cultural codes and challenges. Over time, the sphere of Islamic influence has expanded, and the Internet has come to act as a platform for exchange of personalised understandings of Islam between believing women (and men) globally, not only in the geographic, but also social meaning of the word. The openness of the Muslim women's newsgroups has ensured that the understandings which emerge there are a result of the interaction of different intellectual and cultural contexts, personalities, experiences and modes of study. This is consistent with Ramadan's (2004: 4) observation in regard to global Islam:

Far from media attention, going through the risks of a process of maturation that is necessarily slow, they [Western Muslims] are drawing the shape of European and American Islam: faithful to the principles of Islam, dressed in European and American cultures, and definitively rooted in Western societies. This grassroots movement will soon exert considerable influence over worldwide Islam: in view of globalization and the Westernization of the world, these are the same questions as those already being raised from Morocco to Indonesia.

It is important to note that Ramadan mentions a 'grassroots movement', which signals that Islamic debates have long expanded beyond academia, which, although useful for developing the theory underlying current grassroots Islamic activity, may not be very helpful in marrying theory with practice. The process of change he writes about is two-way, with both majority and minority Muslim contexts affecting the way Islamic principles and their applications can be understood. In the age of digital technologies, this seems to be additionally facilitated by platforms such as Muslim newsgroups where a Moroccan can enter a discussion with an Indonesian.

Moving beyond catchy headline phrases like 'electronic ummah' and 'digital Islam', it is necessary to consider what influence these conversations may have on the contexts where the participants come from and on mainstream Islam, especially in terms of gender. Key to understanding the possibilities for long-lasting influence that women's emerging global interpretations may have, is the concept of Islamic authority. Without women asserting authority over their lives with the help of their knowledge of Islamic principles, gender relationships will remain static and male-defined. However, a critical approach to existing interpretations and solutions, as well as dialogue between varied groups of women, indicate that participants engage with the concept of khilafah at the essence, rather than at the level of manifestation (Barazangi 1996). Here, participants actively decide how their lives will reflect Islamic principles. Bunt (2009) states that analysis of online Islamic authority requires acknowledging the legal diversity and common threads of Muslim thought. The refusal of many participants to follow an Islamic school of thought may be related to their assertion of authority in interpreting the sources themselves.

The different hermeneutic positions, egalitarian, traditionalist and holist, identified in Chapters 3–6 indicate that regardless of views on gender rights and responsibilities, participants entered the online debates and argued to defend and promote their choices and strategies, but also were made aware of others' choices in regard to living their religion. This opportunity, as many participants admitted, empowered them and improved their understanding of the deen. Thus, the activity in the newsgroup may be defined as feminist: by participating, the women there learn not only about Islam, but also about others' views and come to understand them; as no specific views are privileged, women remain relatively flexible in accepting difference and allowing diverse choices to be made.

Participants make sense of their own and other's experiences in two ways, relying on both the Islamic sources, and a pragmatic approach to life. They use both as frameworks of reference, often combining them in an act that constitutes an ultimate merging of theory and practice, something that academic studies are obviously unable to do. Through this, they create lived Islam, a product of individual and group study and reflection. The format of Muslim women's newsgroup discussions, which is asynchronous, additionally facilitates the creation of space for reflection. The opportunity to go in and out of the discussion offers space for developing and testing ideas introduced in the newsgroups in a reflective mode. This merging of different frameworks of reference strikingly dovetails with Ahmed's (2006: 81) observation on women in the early Islamic era:

> they figured things out among themselves and in two ways. They figured them out as they tried to understand their own lives and how to behave and live, talking them over among themselves, interacting with their men, and returning to talk them over in their communities of women. And they figured them out as they listened to the Quran and talked among themselves about what they heard. For this was a culture, at all levels of society and throughout most of the history of Islamic civilization, not of reading but of the common recitation of the Quran. It was ... listened to on all kinds of occasions. ... It was from these together, their own lives and from hearing the words of the Quran, that they formed their sense of the essence of Islam.

The difference between women in early Islam and the participants in this study is that Islam has expanded from the Middle East into all recesses of the world. It is rooted in and defines a number of diverse cultures. The recent development of technology facilitates dialogue between members of other cultures as well as within one's own. Multifaceted collaboration with other participants ensures that they increase their awareness of the diversity within Islam not only in general terms, but on a level of detail that can only be attained in intensive, personal conversations with other individuals who can then explain not only their specific views but also their underlying reasons.

Some feminist scholars state that the private/public binary is an artificial, gendered product of social hierarchies (Karim 2008), strenghtened by the nation-state concept (Reiter 1975; Gailey 1987). It is argued that the idea of public/private space is not neutral as defined by social relations of inclusion and exclusion (Göle 2002). In her critique of the concept of private/public spheres in the context of power structures in Lebanon, Joseph (1997: 75) observes: 'All categories and boundaries are sites of struggle'. Göle (2002) also states that public Islam needs to redefine and recreate the borders of the interior, intimate, illicit gendered space (mahrem)'. This process has already commenced on the part of the participants; some of them contest traditional boundaries which used to define their choices in the past and construct new codes of performance. Online groups are environments where both contestations and affirmations of traditional boundaries take place. Different conceptualizations of Islamically acceptable redefinitions of public and private are expressed in discussions on marriage, sexuality, polygamy, and employment. In the online discussions, women do not contest the public/private binary itself; however, they argue against static understandings of it which define women's functions in society in a very traditional (or 'cultural') way. As in the discussions on gender, in discussions of private and public issues, interpretations of Islamic sources are the framework for these considerations as women contest or affirm social phenomena using arguments based on the Qur'an and Ahadith. The ability to read and understand these texts is integral to participation in the debates. Some women focus on factors other than gender for defining their identity within ummah, such as affiliation within Islam, race, ethnicity, and class. They negotiate the challenges related to these characteristics which arise in varied sociocultural contexts. Their agenda is detailed in Chapter 6 as a counterbalance to the egalitarian-traditionalist binary related to views on gender relations.

This willingness of participants to engage with supporters of different positions has been an unexpected finding, as psychologists suggest that people online tend to gravitate towards like-minded or already known individuals (Bonhard and Sasse 2006). Not so in the case of the Muslim women online – the uniting factors of being a Muslim *and* a woman seem to overweigh the differences in understanding Islam. Even if there is no common agreement among the women, there is certainly a spirit of tolerance and openness. Although some of the discussed issues are non-negotiable, participants do move back on other issues and sometimes reach consensus, which may have important implications for Islamic legislation in the future, as a hadith reports that the Prophet Muhammad said that the Muslim community would never agree upon an error (Janin 2005). Thus, consensus (*ijma*) is the basis of creating new laws.

Although Muslim women participating in the study may take different views on gender, race and class relationships, they also collaborate. Together, and through their discussions on women's roles and responsibilities in various spheres of life, including activities in the overlapping private and public domains, such as marriage, sexuality, polygamy, employment, dress-code, mobility, and sisterhood, they explore divergent models of gender relationships. This multifaceted communication and the fact that Muslim women representing different hermeneutic positions have opened up exchanges among each other are the main findings of this book. Individuals whose views are entirely different and who otherwise would not have encountered and listened to each other are willingly communicating. As the newsgroups are open to *all* Muslim women (and non-Muslim women interested in Islam), the online communities that emerge are very eclectic. In contrast, the literature addressing Muslim women's hermeneutic positions tends to polarise them, suggesting that there are isolated, 'extreme' categories of women: those who have adopted the Islamic framework to challenge patriarchy in Muslim communities, and those who refuse to acknowledge that this patriarchy exists. These binaries overlook the existence of three important factors: that women rarely represent these theoretical formations, with most of them occupying positions in between, moving closer to different ends of the continuum depending on the discussed issue. Second, due to new modes of communication and women's openness, they are no longer isolated. Finally, many women in the newsgroups focus on a combination of issues, where gender relations are only one of the considerations; these women address the configurations of gender, race, ethnicity and class when negotiating solutions to problems discussed online. Throughout, this study further evidences the existence of feminism as a perspective 'embracing diversity, choice and agency within its broad borders' (MacDonald 2007: 201).

This research has been a four-year journey in which I made conscious choices with regard to the literature that I selected as my theoretical framework, the methodology and data production method, the type of data analysis and aspects of the data which I highlighted. As a result, it is a relatively focused study of a very specific context. This means that it does not contain 'generalizable' knowledge, nor is it conclusive. Mellor (2007: 204) wrote that her book had 'omissions, silences and gaps of its own', and this is also the case here. Circumstances and decisions marked the limitations of my book – for example, the fact that I only explored English-speaking newsgroups, and through this excluded non-English speaking women. Some could challenge the categorization I used in the analysis and my use of the term 'Islamic feminism' where participants did not themselves express the wish to use this label. Similarly, I have been questioned at conferences as to why I decided not to include e-mail interviews in the data, as these could have added to the depth of the accounts produced by participants in the discussions. Although my choice of the method of data generation was a result of a conscious decision, I am aware that it closed off some avenues of inquiry.

Women's Islamic discourses evolve, and so does technology. Some participants considered writing a book and mentioned interest from publishers – if they decided to do it together, they could use wikis (web tools facilitating collaborative authoring of texts). Some Muslim women already use social networks such as Facebook and YouTube to communicate their views to society,[1] and sometimes in an ironic and humorous way.[2] It is certain that they will continue using all the technology available to continue this important debate. It is also generally acknowledged that Web 2.0 offers enormous opportunities in terms of interactivity, and the Muslim online environments I mentioned in the introduction to this book are evolving in that direction too (Bunt 2009). I do not believe they will entirely replace newsgroups like the ones addressed in this book, as these are likely to cater to individuals who want to focus on the spiritual purpose of the discussions and the creation of long-lasting bonds with other women, not the technological advancement represented by constantly evolving social networking environments. In December 2008, it was announced that the first virtual world aimed at Muslims called Muxlim Pal was to be launched.[3] Its creator says that its purpose is to facilitate communication and cultivation of shared interests among Muslims. It is also meant to enable non-Muslims interested in Islam and the 'Muslim lifestyle' to learn about different aspects of Muslims' lives. However, it remains an open question, whether such environments are conducive to a critical debate about Islamic issues. They definitely appeal to the young generation of Internet users who manage their social lives through the Internet. Future research may assess their usefulness for the advancement of women's interpretations of Islam.

Notes

1   For example, 'American Muslim Women Speak about the Veil', http://www.youtube.com/watch?v=L85Mcq3EDX8&feature=PlayList&p=89B74 79C37278001&index=0 (accessed on 22 June 2009).
2   For example, 'Top Ten Funniest Things a Muslim Woman Hears', http://www.youtube.com/watch?v=-WduXRIDO3A&feature=PlayList&p=89B74 79C37278001&index=1 (accessed on 22 June 2009).
3   http://news.bbc.co.uk/1/hi/technology/7768601.stm (accessed on 22 June 2009).

Glossary

Ahadith – plural for 'hadith'.

Ayah – Arabic word meaning 'miracle' or 'sign', often used to refer to a single Qur'anic verse.

Dawah – Islamic preaching, or invitation to others to understand Islam through a dialogical process. A person practising dawah may be a religious activist or a community worker.

Fitna – a broad concept denoting disbelief, schism, secession, anarchy and upheaval at once.

Hadith – an account of Prophet Muhammad's saying or action, initially transmitted orally, later collected in books. A hadith consists of two elements: the report of what the Prophet said or did, and a chain of transmitters which documents the route by which a hadith has been transmitted. It also determines the authenticity or weakness of a hadith.

Hijab – a headscarf worn by some Muslim women, sometimes also means modest loose clothing; a 'hijabi' is a hijab wearer. There is a debate whether hijab is an Islamic requirement; some Muslim women wear it as a political statement.

Ijma – consensus on legal issues, gives legitimacy to rulings based on interpretations of Islamic sources. Ijma is regarded by Sunni Muslims as the third source of Islamic law.

Ijtihad – the process of deducting Islamic principles through the interpretation of Islamic sources. Traditionally it has been more significant in the Shi'a school of Islam, as in Sunni Islam relied more on taqlid (imitation). However, in the modern times ijthihad is exercized increasingly often among both Muslim men and women regardless of their Islamic affiliation.

Jihad – an Arabic word meaning 'struggle', it is a religious duty of every Muslim. The Greater Jihad is a personal struggle to improve one's self, intellectually and morally and comprises of jihad against one's self, jihad of the tongue and jihad of the hand; the Lesser Jihad is jihad of the sword and denotes military struggle regulated by Islamic law. Its primary aim is to defend and expand the Islamic state.

Halal – permissible in Islam as based on the Qur'an and the Sunnah. It may refer to behaviour, clothing or food and drink.

Haram – forbidden in Islam as based on the Qur'an and the Sunnah. It may refer to behaviour, clothing or food and drink.

Jilbab – long, loose-fitting garment similar to a coat worn by women

Khimar – everything that is used to cover, conceal; used in the Qur'an in reference to women's obligation to cover their bodies. It is defined by some scholars as a scarf used to cover the head and neck, others argue it means a garment covering the bosom.

Mahram – unmarriageable kin specified in the Qur'an, this includes parents, grandparents, step-parents, siblings, aunts, uncles, nephews, nieces as well as milk-siblings.

Niqab – a type of Islamic dress that includes a face veil, a head-covering and a loose garment, such as a long overcoat; a 'niqabi' is a niqab wearer.

Shahada – Islamic declaration of faith, pronounced three times on conversion: 'There is no god but God, and Muhammad is the Messenger of God'.

Shari'a – Islamic legal system based on the Qur'an, the Sunnah, and classical Islamic jurisprudence: consensus (ijma) and analogy (qiyas) which constitute interpretive law.

Sunnah – an Arabic word lexically meaning 'the road'. It is used to refer to the way (practice) of the Prophet Muhammad, pertaining to belief, religious and social practice, as well as ethics; sometimes used as an adjective, meaning 'in agreement with the Sunnah'.

Surah – an organizational unit (or chapter) of the Qur'an which contains 114 surahs. All the surahs of the Holy Qur'an begin with *Bismillahi 'r-Rahmani 'r-Raham* (in the name of God, the Merciful, the Compassionate). Each surah is named after an incident or purpose, or after a key word in that surah.

Zawj – husband.

Zina – adultery; a haram sexual act that involves sexual intercourse outside of marriage or action that may lead to it. From the legal, shari'a dimension it is a crime that results in a legal penalty.

Bibliography

Abdelatif, Omayama, and Ottaway, Marina (2007) Women in Islamist movements: toward an Islamist model of womens activism. *Carnegie Papers*, No. 2. Available at www.policyarchive.org/bitstream/handle/10207/6449/cmec2_women_in_islam_final1.pdf accessed on 6 July 2009.

Abdul-Rahman, Muhammad S. (2007) *Islam – Questions and Answers. Manners (Part 2)*. London: MSA Publication.

Abdul Rahman, Noor A. (2007) Changing roles, unchanging perceptions and institutions: traditionalism and its impact on women and globalization in Muslim societies in Asia. *The Muslim World*, 97(3).

Abou-Alsamh, Rasheed (2006) Saudi women unveil opinions online. *Christian Science Monitor*, 19 June. Available at: www.csmonitor.com/2006/0619/p06s02-wome.html accessed on 6 July 2009.

Abugideiri, Hibba (2001) The renewed woman of American Islam: shifting lenses toward gender jihad?. *The Muslim World*, 91(1–2).

Abu Romi, Abdel Rahman (2008) Algerias women-only internet café. *IslamOnline*. Available at www.islamonline.net/servlet/Satellite?c=Article_C&cid=1203758091217&pagename=Zone-English-News%2FNWELayout accessed on 21 December 2008.

Afsarudddin, Asma (ed.) (1999) *Hermeneutics and Honor: Negotiating Female Public Space in Islamic/ate Societies*. Cambridge, MA: Harvard University Press.

Afshar, Haleh (ed.) (1985) *Women, Work, and Ideology in the Third World*. London: Routledge.

Afshar, Haleh (ed.) (1993) *Women in the Middle East: Perceptions, Realities and Struggles for Liberation*. Basingstoke: Macmillan.

Afshar, Haleh (1995) Why fundamentalism: Iranian women and their support for Islam. *Women: A Cultural Review*, 6(1).

Afshar, Haleh (1996) *Women and Politics in the Third World*. London: Routledge.

Afshar, Haleh (1998) Strategies of resistance among the Muslim minority in West Yorkshire: impact on women. In N. Charles and H.M. Hinthens (eds), *Gender, Ethnicity and Political Ideologies*. London: Routledge.

Afshar, Haleh (2008) Can I see your hair? Choice, agency, and attitudes: the dilemma of faith and feminism for Muslim women who cover. *Ethnic and Racial Studies*, 31(2).

Ahmad, Aijazuddin and Aijaz, Nasim (1993) From dependency to subordination: Muslim women in the rural setting. In Z.A. Siddiqi and Anwar Jahan Zuberi (eds), *Muslim Women: Problems and Prospects*. Delhi: M.D. Publications.

Ahmad, Fauzia (2001) Modern traditions? British Muslim women and academic achievement. *Gender and Education*, 13(2).

Ahmad, Salbiah (2005) Islam in Malaysia: constitutional and human rights perspectives. *Muslim World Journal of Human Rights*, 2(1).

Ahmed, Leila (1993) *Women and Gender in the Middle East: Historical Roots of a Modern Debate*. Yale, CT: Yale University Press.

Ahmed, Leila (2006) A border passage: from Cairo to America: a womans journey. *Comparative Studies of South Asia, Africa, and the Middle East*, 26(1).

Aidi, Hisham D. (2005) Let us be Moors: Islam, race, and "connected histories". *Souls: A Critical Journal of Black Politics, Culture, and Society*, 7(1).

Alavi, Nasrin (2005) *We Are Iran: The Persian Blogs*. New York: Soft Skull Press.

Al-Hibri, Azizah (1982) A study of Islamic herstory, or how did we ever get into this mess? *Womens Studies International Forum*, 5(2).

Al-Krenawi, Alean et al. (1997) Social work practice with polygamous families. *Child and Adolescent Social Work Journal*. 14(6).

Al-Qaradawi, Yusuf (2007) *Approaching the Sunnah*. Herndon, VA: International Institute of Islamic Thought.

Ali, Tariq (2002) *The Clash of Fundamentalisms: Crusades, Jihads and Modernity*. London: Verso.

Alptekin, Cem (2002) Towards intercultural communicative competence in ELT. *ELT Journal*, 56(1). Available at: http://dzibanche.biblos.uqroo.mx/hemeroteca/elt_journal/2002/enero/560057.pdf accessed on 15 March 2009.

Amason, Allen C. and Schweiger, David M. (1994) Resolving the paradox of conflict, strategic decision making, and organizational performance. *International Journal of Conflict Management*, 5(3).

Amir-Ebrahimi, Masserat (2008a) Blogging from Qom, behind walls and veils. *Comparative Studies of South Asia, Africa and the Middle East*, 28(2).

Amir-Ebrahimi, Masserat (2008b) Transgression in narration: the lives of Iranian women in cyberspace. *Journal of Middle East Womens Studies*, 4(3).

An-Naim, Abdullahi A. (2002) *Islamic Family Law in a Changing World: A Global Resource Book*. London: Zed Books.

Anderson, Jon W. (1999) The internet and Islams new interpreters. In D.F. Eickelman and J.W. Anderson (eds), *New Media in the Muslim World: The Emerging Public Sphere*. Bloomington, IN: Indiana University Press.

Anderson, Jon (2002) , Internet Islam: new media of the Islamic reformation. In D.L. Bowen and E.A. Early (eds), *Everyday Life in the Muslim Middle East*. Bloomington, IN: Indiana University Press.

Armstrong, Karen (2006) *Muhammad: A Prophet for Our Time*. New York: Atlas Books/Harper Collins.

Arnfred, Signe (2003) Sexualities: practices: Sub-Saharan Africa. In S. Joseph and A. Najmabadi (eds), *Encyclopedia of Women and Islamic Cultures: Family, Body, Sexuality, and Health*. Leiden: Brill.

Aronson, Pamela (2003) Feminists or "postfeminists"? Young womens attitudes toward feminism and gender relations. *Gender and Society*, 17(6).

Ayyub, Ruksana (2000) Domestic Violence in the South Asian Muslim Immigrant Population in the United States. *Journal of Social Distress and the Homeless*, 9(3).

Badawi, Jamaal (1995) *Gender Equity in Islam: Basic Principles*. Plainfield, NJ: American Trust.

Badran, Margot (1996) *Feminists, Islam, and Nation*. Princeton, NJ: Princeton University Press.

Badran, Margot (2001a) Locating feminisms: the collapse of secular and religious discourses in the mashriq. *Agenda*, 50.

Badran, Margot (2001b) Understanding Islam, Islamism, and Islamic Feminism. *Journal of Womens History*, 13(1).

Bahramitash, Roksana (2005) The war on terror, feminist orientalism and orientalist feminism: case studies of two North American bestsellers. *Critique: Critical Middle Eastern Studies*. 14(2).

Bakarat, Halim (1993) *The Arab World: Society, Culture, and State*. Berkeley, CA: Univeristy of California Press.

Balchin, Cassandra (2003) With her feet on the ground: women, religion and development in Muslim communities. *Development*, 46(4).

Barak, Azy (2005) Sexual harassment on the internet. *Social Science Computer Review*, 23(1).

Barazangi, Nimat Hafez (1996) Viceregency and gender justice in Islam. In N.H. Barazangi, M.R. Zaman and O. Afzal (eds), *Islamic Identity and the Struggle for Justice*. Gainesville, FL: University of Florida Press.

Barazangi, Nimat Hafez (2004) *Womans Identity and the Qur'an: A New Reading*. Gainesville, FL: University of Florida Press.

Barlas, Asma (2004) The Qur'an, sexual equality, and feminism. Available at: www.asmabarlas.com/TALKS/20040112_UToronto.pdf accessed on 15 March 2009.

Barlas, Asma (2006) *"Believing Women" in Islam: Unreading Patriarchal Interpretations of the Qurān*. Austin, TX: University of Texas Press.

Bastani, Susan (2001) Muslim women online. *Arab World Geographer*, 3(1).

Baudrillard, Jean (1967) Review of Marshall McLuhans *"Understanding Media"*. *L'Homme et la Société*, 5.

BBC Radio Four (2008) Interview with Parasto Dokoohaki, 15 December. Available at: www.bbc.co.uk/radio4/womanshour/04/2008_51_mon.shtml accessed on 6 July 2009.

Beck, Ulrich and Cronin, Ciaran (2006) *The Cosmopolitan Vision*. Cambridge: Polity.

Benthal, Jonathan and Bellion-Jourdan Jerome (2003) *The Charitable Crescent: Politics of Aid in the Muslim World*. London: IB Tauris.

Bickel, Beverly (2003) Weapons of magic: Afghan women asserting voice via the net. *Journal of Computer-Mediated Communication*, 8(3). Available at: http://jcmc.indiana.edu/vol8/issue2/bickel.html accessed on 15 March 2009.

Bhabha, Homi (1994) *The Location of Culture*. Abingdon: Routledge.

Bhimji, Fazila (2005) "Assalam u alaikum: Brother I have a right to my opinion on this": British Islamic women assert their positions in virtual space. In A. Jule (ed.) *Gender and Language Use in Religious Identity*. London: Palgrave Macmillan.

Blank, Grant (2008) Online research methods and social theory. In N. Fielding, R. Lee and G. Blank (eds.), *The Handbook of Online Research Methods*. Thousands Oaks, CA: Sage.

Bonhard, P. and Sasse, M. A. (2006) "Knowing me, knowing you": using profiles and social networking to improve recommender systems. *BT Technology Journals*, 24(3).

boyd, danah (2009) A reponse to Christine Hine in Anette N. Markham and Nancy K. Boyd (eds), *Internet Inquiry: Conversations about Method*. London: Sage.

Bradley Hagerty, Barbara (2008) Some Muslims in US quietly engage in polygamy. *National Public Radio*, 28 May. Available at: www.npr.org/templates/story/story.php?storyId=90857818 accessed on 2 July 2009.

Brah, Avtar (1993) Race and culture in the gendering of labour markets: South Asian young Muslim women and the labour market. *New Community*, 19(3).

Brah, Avtar (1994) "Race" and "culture" in the gendering of labour markets: South Asian young muslim women and the labour market. In M. Maynard and H. Afshar (eds.), *The Dynamics of Race and Gender*. London: Taylor & Francis.

Brend, Barbara (1991) *Islamic Art*. Cambridge, MA: Harvard University Press.

Brayton, Jennifer (1997) What makes feminist research feminist? The structure of feminist research within the social sciences. Available at: www.unb.ca/PARL/win/femininmethod.htm accessed on 15 May 2007.

Brooks, Geraldine (1995) *Nine Parts of Desire: The Hidden World of Islamic Women*. New York: Anchor Books.

Brouwer, Lenie (2004) Dutch-Muslims on the internet: a new discussion platform. *Journal of Muslim Minority Affairs*, 24(1).

Brouwer, Lenie (2006) Giving voice to Dutch Moroccan girls on the internet. *Global Media Journal*, 5(9). Available at: http://lass.calumet.purdue.edu/cca/gmj/fa06/gmj_fa06_brouwer.htm accessed on 17 December 2008.

Bullock, Katherine (2002) *Rethinking Muslim Women and the Veil: Challenging Historical and Modern Stereotypes*. Herndon, VA: International Institute of Islamic Thought.

Bullock, Katherine (2005) *Muslim Women Activists in North America: Speaking for Ourselves*. Austin, TX: University of Texas Press.

Burns, Karima (2001) *Questions and Answers on Natural Health*. Available at: www.islamonline.net/english/Science/2001/02/article19.shtml accessed on 6 July 2009.

Bunt, Gary (2000) *Virtually Islamic: Computer-mediated Communication and Cyber Islamic Environments*. Lampeter: University of Wales Press.

Bunt, Gary (2003) *Islam in the Digital Age: E-jihad, Online Fatwas and Cyber Islamic environments*. London: Pluto Press.

Bunt, Gary (2009) *iMuslims: Rewiring the House of Islam*. Chapel Hill, NC: University of Carolina Press.

Camara, Fatou K. (2007) Women and the law: a critique of Senegalese family law. *Social Identities*, 13(6).

Caspi, Avner, and Gorsky, Paul (2006) Online deception: prevalence, motivation, and emotion. *CyberPsychology & Behavior*, 9(1).

Castells, Manuel (2004) *The Power of Identity, the Information Age: Economy, Society and Culture*. Cambridge, MA: Blackwell.

Cesari, Jocelyne (2004) *When Islam and Democracy Meet: Muslims in Europe and in the United States*. Basingstoke: Palgrave Macmillan.

Chulov, Martin (2009) Its ok to use women for suicide bombings. *Mail and Guardian*, 15 November. Available at: http://www.mg.co.za/article/2008-11-15-its-ok-to-use-women-for-suicide-bombings accessed 29 June 2009.

Clare, Judith and Hamilton, Helen (2003) *Writing Research: Transforming Data into Text*. Oxford: Elsevier.

Clark, Janine A. (2004) *Islam, Charity, and Activism*. Bloomington, IN: Indiana University Press.

cooke, miriam (2002) Islamic feminism before and after September 11th, *Duke Journal of Gender Law and Policy*, 9.

cooke, miriam (2007) The Muslimwoman. *Contemporary Islam*, 1(2).

Crowley, Sharon, and Hawhee, Debra (1999) *Ancient Rhetorics for Contemporary Students*. Berkeley, CA: University of California Press.

Daily Telegraph (2008) Iranian female bloggers get dress code threats, 27 April. Available at: www.telegraph.co.uk/news/worldnews/middleeast/iran/1904328/Irans-female-bloggers-get-dress-code-threats.html accessed on 6 July 2009.

Dale, Angela et al. (2002) Routes into education and employment for young Pakistani and Bangladeshi women in the UK. *Ethnic and Racial Studies*. 25(6).

Dangor, Suleman (2001) Historical perspective, current literature and an opinion survey among Muslim women in contemporary South Africa: a case Study. *Journal of Muslim Minority Affairs*, 21(1).

De Dreu, Carsten and Weingart, Laurie R. (2003) Task versus relationship conflict, team performance, and team member satisfaction: a meta-analysis. *Journal of Applied Psychology*, 88(4).

Dolowitz, David, Buckley, Steve, and Sweeney, Fionnghuala (2008) *Researching Online*. London: Palgrave Macmillan.

Donath, Judith S. (1998) Identity and deception in the virtual community. In M.A. Smith, and P. Kollock (eds) *Communities in Cyber Space*. London: Routledge.

Donath, Judith S. (1999) Visualizing conversation. *Journal of Computer Mediated Communication*, 4(4). Available at: http://jcmc.indiana.edu/vol4/issue4/donath.html accessed on 3 July 2009.

Douglass, Susan L. and Shaikh, Munir A. (2004) Defining Islamic education: differentiation and applications. *Current Issues in Comparative Education*, 7(1).

Douki, Saida and Nacef, Fathy (2002) Womens mental health in Tunisia. *World Psychiatry*, 1(1).

Dunne, Bruce (1998) Power and sexuality in the Middle East. *Middle East Report*, 206.

Echols, A. (1989) *Daring to Be Bad: Radical Feminism in America, 1967–1975*. Minneapolis, MN: University of Minnesota Press.

Edmunds, June, and Turner, Bryan S. (2005) Global generations: social change in the twentieth century. *The British Journal of Sociology*, 56(4).

Eickelman, Dale F. (1999) The coming transformation of the Muslim world. *Middle East Review of International Affairs*, 3(3).

Eickelman, Dale F. and Anderson, Jon W. (eds) (1999) *New Media in the Muslim World: The Emerging Public Sphere*. Bloomington, IN: Indiana University Press.

El-Azhary Sonbol, Amira (2003) *Women of Jordan*. Syracuse, NY: Syracuse University Press.

Eldon, Eric (2007) Religious social networks on the rise. *Venture Beat*, 18 September. Available at: http://venturebeat.com/2007/09/18/religious-social-networks-on-the-rise/ accessed on 6 July 2009.

El Guindi, Fadwa (1999a) *Veil: Modesty, Privacy and Resistance*. Oxford: Berg.

El Guindi, Fadwa (1999b) Veiling resistance. *Fashion Theory*, 3(1).

El-Sanabary, Nagat (1994) Female education in Saudi Arabia and the reproduction of gender division. *Gender and Education*. 6(2).

Engineer, Asghar Ali (2007) *Islam in Contemporary World*. New Delhi: Sterling.

Esposito, John and Voll, John Obert (1996) *Islam and Democracy*. Cambridge, MA: Oxford University Press.

Esposito, John, E. (2002) *What Everyone Needs to Know about Islam*. Cambridge, MA: Oxford University Press.

Esposito, John E. and Burgat, François (2003) *Modernizing Islam: Religion in the Public Sphere in the Middle East and Europe*. London: Hurst.

Ess, Charles and Jones, Steven (2004) Ethical decision-making and internet research: recommendations from the AoIR Ethics Working Committee. In E.A. Buchanan (ed.), *Readings in Virtual Research Ethics*. Hershey, PA: Idea Group.

Eynon, Rebecca, Fry, Jenny and Schroeder, Ralph (2008) The ethics of online research. In N. Fielding, R. Lee and G. Blank (eds) *The Handbook of Online Research Methods*. Thousand Oaks, CA: Sage.

Fahy, Patrick J. (2007) Ethics review concerns of Canadas distance researchers. In U. Demiray and R. Sharma (eds), *Ethical Practices and Implications in Distance Learning*. Hershey, PA: IGI Global.

Falah, Ghazi-Walid (2005) *Geographies of Muslim Women: Gender, Religion, and Space*. New York: Guilford Press.

Farooq, Mohammad O. (2006) *Islamic Law and the Use and Abuse of Hadith*. Available at: http://www.globalwebpost.com/farooqm/writings/islamic/law_hadith.doc accessed on 20 July 2009.

Fielding, Nigel, Lee, Raymond and Blank, Grant (2008) *The Handbook of Online Research Methods*. Thousand Oaks, CA: Sage.

Firth, Sarah (2008) Women-only taxi firm sets up. *This Is Notthingam*, 16 October. Available at: http://www.thisisnottingham.co.uk/transport/Women-taxi-firm-sets/article-402757-detail/article.html accessed on 5 July 2009.

Franks, Myfanwy (2000) Crossing the borders of whiteness? White Muslim women who wear the *Hijab* in Britain today. *Ethnic and Racial Studies*, 23(5).

Franks, Myfanwy (2001) *Women and Revivalism in the West: Choosing Fundamentalism in a Liberal Democracy*. Basingstoke: Palgrave.

Gailey, Christine Ward (1987) *Kinship to Kingship: Gender Hierarchy and State Formation in the Tongan Islands*. Austin, TX: University of Texas Press.

Gerami, Shahin (1995) *Women and Fundamentalism: Islam and Christianity*. New York: Routledge.

Giacaman, Rita (1988) *Life and Health in Three Palestinian Villages*. London: Ithaca.

Gorelick, Sherry (1991) Contradictions of feminist methodology. *Gender & Society*, 5(4).

Göle, Nilüfer (1996) *The Forbidden Modern: Civilization and Veiling*. Ann Arbor, MI: University of Michigan Press.

Göle, Nilüfer (1997) The gendered nature of the public space. *Public Culture*, 10(1).

Göle, Nilüfer (2002) Islam in public: new visibilities and new imaginaries. *Public Culture*, 14(1).

Górak-Sosnowska, K. (2007) Perception and misperception of Islam in Polish textbooks. *Rocznik Orientalistyczny (Annual of Oriental Studies)* 60(1).

Grandea, Nona, and Kerr, Joanna (1998) Frustrated and displaced: Filipina domestic workers in Canada. *Gender and Development*, 6(1).

Griffin, Wendy (2004) The goddess net. In L. Dawson and D. Cowan (eds), *Religion Online*. London: Routledge.

Hacinebioglu, Ismail L. (2007) A methodological approach to the epistemic classification of knowledge in religious sciences, *Journal of Beliefs & Values: Studies in Religion & Education*, 28(3).

Haddad, Yvonne Y. (1997) A century of Islam in America. *Hamdard Islamicus: Quarterly Journal of Studies and Research in Islam*, 21(4).

Haddad, Yvonne Y., Smith, Jane I., and Moore, Kathleen M. (2006) *Muslim Women in America: the Challenge of Islamic Identity Today*. New York: Oxford University Press.

Hafez, Sherine (2003) *The Terms of Empowerment*. Cairo: The American University in Cairo Press.

Halstead, Mark (2004) An Islamic concept of education. *Comparative Education*, 40(4).

Harding, Sandra (ed.) (1987) *Feminism and Methodology: Social Science Issues*. Bloomington: Indiana University Press.

Hassan, Riffat (1988) Equal before Allah? Woman-man equality in the Islamic tradition. *Women Living Under Muslim Laws Dossier*, 5–6.

Hassan, Riffat (1995) Rights of women within Islamic communities. *Canadian Womens Studies*, 15(2–3).

Hassan, Riffat (2000) Is family planning permitted by Islam?. In G. Webb (ed.), *Windows of Faith: Muslim Women Scholar-Activists in North America*. Syracuse, NY: Syracuse University Press.

Hassan, Riffat (2001) Challenging the stereotypes of fundamentalism: an Islamic feminist perspective. *The Muslim World*, 91(1–2).

Hassan, Riffat (2004) Are human rights compatible with Islam? The issue of the rights of women in Muslim communities. *The Religious Consultation on Population, Reproductive Health and Ethics*. Available at: http://www.webb-international.org/download/word/articles_riffat/AreHumanRightsCompatiblewithIslam.doc accessed on 2 July 2009.

Hassouneh-Phillips, Dena (2001a) Polygamy and wife abuse: a qualitative study of Muslim women in America. *Health Care for Women International*, 22(8).

Hassouneh-Phillips, Dena (2001b) American Muslim women's experiences of leaving abusive relationships. *Health Care for Women International*, 22(4).

Hawker, R.W. (2002) Imagining a Bedouin past: stereotypes and cultural representation in the contemporary UAE. *Beirut Institute for Media Arts Conference*. Available at: http://inhouse.lau.edu.lb/bima/papers/R_W_Hawker.pdf accessed on 1 July 2009.

Heaton, Tim (2003) Socioeconomic and familial status of women associated with age at first marriage in three Islamic societies. In D. Cheal (ed.), *Family*. London: Routledge.

Henry, Astrid (2004) *Not My Mothers Sister*. Bloomington, IN: Indiana University Press.

Herman, Didi (1994) *Rights of Passage: Struggles for Lesbian and Gay Legal Equality*. Toronto: University of Toronto Press.

Hermida, Alfred (2002) Web gives a voice to Iranian women. *BBC News*, 17 June. Available at: http://news.bbc.co.uk/1/hi/sci/tech/2044802.stm accessed on 6 July 2009.

Hijab, Nadia (1988) *Womanpower*. Cambridge: Cambridge University Press.

Hirschkind, Charles (2001) The ethics of listening: Cassette-Sermon audition in contemporary Egypt. *American Ethnologist*, 28(3).

Ho, Shirley S., Lee, Waipeng and Sahul Hameed, Shahiraa (2008) Muslim surfers on the internet: using the theory of planned behaviour to examine the factors influencing engagement in online religious activities. *New Media Society*, 10(1).

Ho, Christina and Dreher,Tanja (2009) Not another hijab row: new conversations on gender, race, religion and the making of communities. *International Feminist Journal of Politics*, 11(1).

Hitchens, Christopher (2008) Introduction. In A.H. Ali (ed.), *Infidel: My Life*. New York: Free Press.

Hooshmand, Parvaneh (2003) Sexualities: practices: Iran. In S. Joseph and A. Najmabadi (eds) *Encyclopedia of Women and Islamic Cultures: Family, Body, Sexuality, and Health*. Leiden: Brill.

Hussein, Aqeel and McElroy, Damien (2008) Mother of all suicide bombers warns of rise in attacks. *The Daily Telegraph*, 15 November. Available at: http://www.telegraph.co.uk/news/worldnews/middleeast/iraq/3464411/Mother-of-all-suicide-bombers-warns-of-rise-in-attacks.html accessed 11 July 2009.

Hyder, Syed Akbar (2008) *Reliving Karbala: Martyrdom in South Asian Memory*. Cambridge, MA: Oxford University Press US.

Imtoual, Alia, and Hussein, Shakira (2009) Challenging the myth of the happy celibate: Muslim women negotiating contemporary relationships. *Contemporary Islam*, 3(1).

Jackson, Linda A., Ervin, Kelly S., Gardner, Philip D. and Schmitt, Neal (2001) Gender and the internet: women communicating and men searching. *Sex Roles*, 44(5–6).

Janin, Hunt (2005) *The Pursuit of Learning in the Islamic World*, Jefferson, NC: McFarland.

Jehn, Karen A. (1997) A quantitative analysis of conflict types and dimensions in organizational groups. *Administrative Science Quarterly*, 42.

Johns, Mark D., Chen, Shing-Ling S. and Hall, G. (2004) *Online Social Research: Methods, Issues, and Ethics*. New York: Peter Lang.

Jordan, Brigitte, and Henderson, Austin (1995) Interaction analysis: foundations and practice. *Journal of the Learning Sciences*, 4(1).

Joseph, Suad (1997) The public/private – the imagined boundary in the imagined nation/state/community: The Lebanese case. *Feminist Review*, 57(1).

Kandiyoti, Deniz (1988) Bargaining with patriarchy. *Gender & Society*, 2(3).

Kapiszewski, Andrzej (2006) Saudi Arabia: steps toward democratization or reconfiguration of authoritarianism? *Journal of Asian and African Studies*, 41(5–6).

Karam, Azza (1998) *Women, Islamisms and the State: Contemporary Feminisms in Egypt*. Houndmills: Macmillan.

Karim, Jamillah (2008) *American Muslim Women*. New York: New York University Press.

Karim, Jamillah (2005) Voices of faith, faces of beauty: connecting American Muslim women through *Azizah*. In m. cooke and B. Lawrence (eds), *Muslim Networks: From Hajj to Hip Hop*. Cape Hill, NC: University of North Carolina Press.

Karmani, Sohail (2003) Islam, English and 9/11: an interview with Alastair Pennycook. *TESOL Islamia*. Available at: http://www.tesolislamia.org/ articles/interview_ap.pdf accessed on 2 March 2009.

Katz, Marion Holmes (2008) Womens Mawlid perfomances in Sanaa and the construction of 'Popular Islam'. *International Journal of Middle Eastern Studies*, 40.

Khan, Shahnaz (2000) *Muslim Women: Crafting a North American Identity*. Gainesville, FL: University of Florida Press.

Khan, Shahnaz (2002) *Aversion and Desire: Negotiating Muslim Female Identity in the Diaspora*. London: Womens Press.

King, Storm A. (1996) Researching internet communities: proposed ethical guidelines for reporting of results. *The Information Society: An International Journal*. 12(2).

Kochuyt, Thierry (2009) God, gifts, and poor people: on charity in Islam. *Social Compass*, 56(1).

Kupferberg, Irit and Green, David (2005) *Troubled Talk*. Berlin: Walter de Gruyter.

Lee, Rebekah (2002) Understanding African womens conversion to Islam: Cape Town in Perspective. *Annual Review of Islam in South Africa*, 5. Available at: http://web.uct.ac.za/depts/religion/documents/ARISA/2002_P4_Lee.pdf accessed 2 July 2009.

Lewins, Ann, and Silver, Christina (2007) *Using Software in Qualitative Research*. London: Sage.

Lewis, Bernard (1985) The crows of the Arabs. *Critical Inquiry*, 12(1).

Li, Qing (2006) Computer-mediated communication: a meta-analysis of male and female attitudes and behaviors. *International Journal on E-learning*, 5(4).

Lincoln, Yvonna S. and Guba, Egon G. (1985) *Naturalistic Inquiry*. Newbury Park, CA: Sage.

Luff, Donna (1999) Dialogue across the divides: 'moments of rapport' and power in feminist reseach with anti-feminist women. *Sociology*, 33(4).

MacDonald, Laura Zahra (2007) *Islamic Feminisms*. Unpublished Doctoral Book, University of York.

McLuhan, Marshall (1987) *Understanding Media: The Extensions of Man.* London: Ark Paperbacks.

McRobbie, Angela (1982) The politics of feminist research: between talk, text and action. *Feminist Review,* 12.

Makoni, Sinfree and Pennycook, Alastair (2005) Disinventing and (re)constituting languages. *Critical Inquiry in Language Studies*, 2(3).

Malhotra, Anju (1991) Gender and changing generational relations: spouse choice in Indonesia. *Demography*, 28(4).

Mallick, Seeme, and Naghmana, Ghani (2005) A review of the relationship between poverty, population growth, and environment. *The Pakistan Development Review*, 44(4). Available at: http://www.pide.org.pk/pdf/ PDR/2005/Volume4/597-614.pdf accessed on 12 August 2009.

Mandaville, Peter (2007) *Global Political Islam*. London: Routledge.

Mann, Chris and Stewart, Fiona (2000) *Internet Communication and Qualitative Research*. London: Sage.

Markham, Annette N. (2004) Representation in online ethnographies: a matter of context sensitivity. In M.D. Johns, S. Chen and G. Hall (eds), *Online Social Research: Methods, Issues, and Ethics*. New York: Peter Lang.

Markham, Anette N. and Baym, Nancy, K. (eds) (2009) *Internet Inquiry: Conversations about Method*. London: Sage.

Mason, Jennifer (2002) *Qualitative Researching*. London: Sage.

Mayer, Ann Elizabeth (1995) Womens rights: reflections on the Middle Eastern Experience. In J.S. Peters and A. Wolper (eds), *Womens Rights, Human Rights*. London: Routledge.

Mayer, Ann Elizabeth (1996) Reform of personal status laws in North Africa: A Problem of Islamic or Mediterranean laws? *Middle East Journal*, 49(3).

Mejia, Melanie P. (2007) Gender *Jihad*: Muslim women, Islamic jurisprudence, and womens rights. *Kritikē*, 1(1).

Mellor, Jody (2007) *Parallel Lives? Working-class Muslim and Non-Muslim Women at University*. Unpublished Doctoral Book, University of York.

Mernissi, Fatima (1985) *Beyond the Veil: Male-Female Dynamics in Muslim Society*. London: Al Saqi Books.

Mernissi, Fatima (1992) *The Veil and the Male Elite: a Feminist Interpretation of Womens Rights in Islam*. New York: Basic Books.

Mernissi, Fatima (2001) *Sheherazade Goes West: Different Cultures, Different Harems*. New York: Washington Square Press.

Mies, Maria (1983) Towards a methodology of feminist research. In G. Bowles, and R. Duelli-Klein (eds), *Theories of Womens Studies*. London: Routledge.

Moghissi, Haideh (1999) *Feminism and Islamic Fundamentalism: The Limits of Postmodern Analysis.* London: Zed Press.

Mohd-Asraf, Ratnawati (2005) English and Islam: a clash of civilizations? *Journal of Language Identity and Education.* 4(2).

Morris, Merrill, and Ogan, Christine (1996) The internet as mass medium. *Journal of Communication,* 46(1).

Muecke, Douglas C. (1980) *The Compass of Irony.* London: Routledge.

Nanji, Azim and Nanji, Razia (2008) *Dictionary of Islam.* London: Penguin Books.

Nasr, Seyyed Hossein (1987) *Traditional Islam in the Modern World.* London: Taylor & Francis.

Nauck, Bernhard, and Klaus, Daniela (2005) Families in Turkey. In Bert N. Adams and Jan Trost (eds) *Handbook of World Families.* London: Sage.

Nieuwerk, Karen Van (2006) *Women Embracing Islam: Gender and Conversion in the West.* Austin, TX: University of Texas Press.

Niva, Steve (1998) Between clash and co-optation: US foreign policy and the specter of Islam. *Middle East Report,* 208(3).

Noorani, Abdul G. (2002) *Islam and Jihad: Prejudice Versus Reality.* London: Palgrave Macmillan.

Olivero, Nadia, and Lunt, Peter (2004) When the ethics is functional to the method: the case of e-mail aualitative interviews. In E.A. Buchanan (ed.), *Readings in Virtual Research Ethics.* Hershey, PA: Idea Group.

Oni, Jacob Bamidele (1996) Qualitative exploration of intra-household variations in treatment of child illness in polygynous Yoruba families: the use of local expressions. *Health Transition Review,* 6.

Orgocka, Aida (2004) Perceptions of communication and education about sexuality among Muslim immigrant girls in the US. *Sex Education: Sexuality, Society and Learning,* 4(3).

Ouedghiri, Meryem (2002) Writing womens bodies on the palimpset of Islamic history: Fatima Mernissi and Assia Djebar. *Cultural Dynamics,* 14(7).

Palfreyman, David, and Al-Khalili, Muhamed (2003) ASCII-ized Gulf Arabic. *Journal of Computer-Mediated Communication,* 9(1).

Parker-Jenkins, Marie (2002) Equal access to state funding: the case of Muslim schools in Britain. *Race Ethnicity and Education,* 5(3).

Pelletreau, Robert H. (1996) Dealing with the Muslim Politics of the Middle East: Algeria, Hamas, Iran. Available at: http://dosfan.lib.uic.edu/ERC/bureaus/nea/960508PelletreauMuslim.html accessed on 30 November 2009.

Pinn, Irmgard (2000) From exotic harem beauty to Islamic fundamentalist: Women in Islam. In K. Hafez and M.A. Kenny (eds), *The Islamic World and the West: an Introduction to Political Cultures and International Relations.* Leiden: Brill.

Rahimi, Babak (2008) The politics of the internet in Iran. In M. Semati (ed.), *Media, Culture and Society in Iran.* London: Routledge.

Rahman, Fazlur (1980) *Islam: Ideology and the Way of Life*. London: Muslim Schools Trust.

Ramadan, Tariq (1999) *To Be a European Muslim*. Leicester: The Islamic Foundation.

Ramadan, Tariq (2004) *Western Muslims and the Future of Islam*. New York: Oxford University Press.

Ramazanoğlu, Caroline, and Holland, Janet (2002) *Feminist Methodology: Challenges and Choices*. London: Sage.

Rashid, Sabina Faiz (2003) Sexualities: practices: South Asia. In S. Joseph and A. Najmabadi (eds), *Encyclopedia of Women and Islamic Cultures: Family, Body, Sexuality, and Health*. Leiden: Brill.

Read, Jennan Ghazal (2003) The sources of gender role attitudes among Christian and Muslim Arab-American women. *Sociology of Religion*, 64(2).

Reiter, Rayna (1975) Men and women in the South of France: public and private domains. In G. Rubin and R. Reiter (eds), *Toward an Anthropology of Women*. New York: Monthly Review Press.

Richardson, Gail (2004) Islamic Law and Zakat: Waqf resources in Pakistan. In S. Heyneman (ed.) *Islam and Social Policy*. Nashville, TN: Vanterbilt University Press.

Roald, Sophie Anne (2001) *Women in Islam: the Western Experience*. London: Routledge.

Roy, Oliver (2004) *Globalised Islam: the Search for a New Ummah*. London: Hurst & Co.

Sachedina, Zulie (1990) Islam, procreation, and the law. *International Family Planning Perspectives*, 16(3).

Safi, Omid (2003) *Progressive Muslims: on Justice, Gender, and Pluralism*. Oxford: Oneworld.

Said, Edward (1979) *Orientalism*. New York: Vintage.

Sæverås Elin Finnseth (2003) *Femail Genital Mutilation: Understanding Issues*. Available at: http://ec.europa.eu/justice_home/daphnetoolkit/files/projects/2003_028/int_understanding_the_issue_fgm_report_norway.pdf accessed 22 April 2009.

Secor, Anna J. (2002) The veil and urban space in Istanbul: womens dress, mobility and Islamic knowledge. *Gender, Place & Culture: A Journal of Feminist Geography*, 9(1).

Shaheed, Farida (1986) The cultural articulation of patriarchy: legal systems, Islam and women. *South Asia Bulletin*, 6(1).

Shehada, Nahda (2009) House of obedience: social norms, individual agency, and historical contingency. *Journal of Middle East Womens Studies*, 5(1).

Sherif, Bahira (1999) The prayer of a married man is equal to seventy prayers of a single man: the central role of marriage among upper-middle-class Muslim Egyptians. *Journal of Family Issues*, 20(5).

Skalli, Loubna H. (2006) Communicating gender in the public sphere: women and information technologies in the MENA. *Journal of Middle East Womens Studies*, 2(3).

Sly, F. *et al.* (1999) Trends in the labour market participation of ethnic groups. In *Labour Market Trends.* London: Highbury House Communications.

Souaiaia, Ahmed E. (2007) Reasoned and inspired beliefs: a study of Islamic theology. *The Muslim World*, 97(2).

Souaiaia, Ahmed E. (2008) *Contesting Justice: Women, Islam, Law, and Society.* Albany, NY: State University of New York Press.

Spivak, Gayatri C. (1988) *In Other Worlds: Essays in Cultural Politics.* New York: Routledge.

Şentürk, Ömer F. (2008) *Charity in Islam: A Comprehensive Guide to Zakat.* Somerset, NJ: Tughra Books.

Talhami, Ghada Hashem (2001) Whither the social network of Islam. *The Muslim World*, 91(3–4).

Taylor, Tayyibah (2003) How media forms perceptions. Speech given at a Muslim Womens League of America event, available at: http://www.mwlusa.org/topics/media/mediaperceptions.htm accessed on 25 July 2009.

Thomas, Jim (2004) Reexamining the ethics of internet research: facing the challenge of overzealous oversight. In M.D. Johns, S. Chen and G. Hall (eds), *Online Social Research: Methods, Issues, and Ethics.* New York: Peter Lang.

Tohidi, Nayereh (2003) *Middle Eastern Women on the Move.* Washington, DC: Woodrow Wilson International Center for Scholars.

Touray, Isatou (2006) Sexuality and womens sexual rights in Gambia. *IDS Bulletin*, 37(5).

Turkle, Sherry (1995) *Life on the Screen: Identity in the Age of Internet.* New York: Simon & Schuster.

Twenge, Jean M. (1997) "Mrs. his name": womens preferences for married names. *Psychology of Women Quarterly*, 21(3).

Varisco, Daniel (2005) *Islam Obscured: The Rhetoric of Anthropological Representation.* London: Palgrave Macmillan.

Varnhagen, Connie K. *et al.* (2005) How informed is online informed consent?. *Ethics & Behavior*, 15(1).

Valsiner, Jaan (1989) *Child Development in a Cultural Context.* Ann Arbor, MN: University of Michigan Press.

Visser, Tirza (2002) Islam, gender, and reconciliation: making room for new gender perspectives. In J.D. Gort *et al.* (eds), *Religion, Conflict, and Reconciliation.* Amsterdam: Rodopi.

Wadud, Amina (1999) *Qur'an and Woman: Rereading the Sacred Text from a Womans Perspective.* Cambridge, MA: Oxford University Press.

Wadud, Amina (2000) Alternative Qur'anic interpretation and the status of Muslim women. In G. Webb (ed.) *Windows of Faith: Muslim Women Scholar-Activists in North America.* Syracuse, NY: Syracuse University Press.

Wadud, Amina (2005) Citizenship and faith. In M. Friedman (ed.), *Women and Citizenship*. Cambridge, MA: Oxford University Press US.

Wadud, Amina (2006) *Inside the Gender Jihad: Womens Reform in Islam*. Oxford: Oneworld.

Waris Maqsood, Ruyaiyyah (nd), Islam, culture, and women. *Islam for Today*. Available at: http://www.islamfortoday.com/ruqaiyyah09.htm accessed on 1 July 2009.

Waris Maqsood, Ruqaiyyah (1998) *Living Islam: Treading the Path of the Ideal*. New Delhi: Goodword Books.

Weiss, Anita M. (1994) Challenges for Muslim Women in a Postmodern World. In A.S. Akbar and H. Donnan (eds), *Islam, Globalisation and Postmodernity*. London: Routledge.

Weller, Paul *et al.* (2001) *Religious Discrimination in England and Wales*. Home Office Research, Development and Statistics Directorate. http://www.homeoffice.gov.uk/rds/pdfs/hors220.pdf accessed on 25 July 2009.

Williams, Raymond (1975) *Television: Technology and Cultural Form*. New York: Schocken Books.

Williams, Rachel, and Wittig, Michele A. (2008) 'I'm not a feminist, but … factors contributing to the discrepancy between pro-feminist orientation and feminist social identity. *Sex Roles*, 37(11–12).

Witmer, Diane F. and Katzman, Sandra L. (1997) On-line smiles: does gender make a difference in the use of graphic accents? *Journal of Computer-Mediated Communication*, 2(4).

Worth, Robert (2009) Better sex: with help from the Qur'an. *The Observer*, 5 July.

Zaman, Saminaz (2008) From imam to cyber-mufti: consuming identity in Muslim America. *The Muslim World*, 98(4).

Zeitzen, Miriam, K. (2008) *Polygamy: A Cross-Cultural Analysis*. Oxford: Berg.

Zelez, Paul Tiymbe (2005) Banishing the silences: towrds the globalization of African history. *1st General Assembly of CODESRIA*, http://www.codesria.org/Links/conferences/general_assembly11/papers/zeleza.pdf accessed on 2 July 2009.

Index